C000130140

VANISHED
DOWNTOWN
HARTFORD

VANISHED
DOWNTOWN
HARTFORD

DANIEL STERNER

THE
History
PRESS

Published by The History Press
Charleston, SC 29403
www.historypress.net

Copyright © 2013 by Daniel Sterner
All rights reserved

Back cover, bottom: Hartford Collection, Hartford History Center, Hartford Public Library.

First published 2013

Manufactured in the United States

ISBN 978.1.60949.895.5

Library of Congress CIP data applied for.

Notice: The information in this book is true and complete to the best of our knowledge. It is offered without guarantee on the part of the author or The History Press. The author and The History Press disclaim all liability in connection with the use of this book.

All rights reserved. No part of this book may be reproduced or transmitted in any form whatsoever without prior written permission from the publisher except in the case of brief quotations embodied in critical articles and reviews.

The building which is going on in this city this Spring gives abundant assurance of the prosperity of our city. Parish is building, on State street, a fine block of stone buildings on the site of the old rookery which has been a hissing and a by-word for years. Mr. Pond is making similar improvements near Exchange Corner and next to the City Bank. The pickaxes have commenced hatcheting the earth west of the Allyn House, preparatory to the erection of Mr. Allyn's new block and hall. Old stores are undergoing a process of rejuvenation, merchants are tearing down and building greater, dwellings spring up in all directions, and Hartford is keeping time with the fast age in which we live. "Push on your column!"

—*Hartford Courant*, April 9, 1860

If it took only as long to put up buildings as it does to tear them down, Hartford might have her Atheneum addition in almost less time than it takes to tell it, and city blocks in scarce a longer time than it takes to say "Jack Robinson." The most cherished of our landmarks which have taken years to erect, may be dismantled so quick that it would pay the moving picture men to be on hand with their machines and snap the whole operation.

—*Hartford Courant*, "Preparing for New Atheneum Addition," July 11, 1907

CONTENTS

ACKNOWLEDGEMENTS

For their assistance in providing me with photographs and other materials for this project, I would like to thank Tomas Nenortas of the Hartford Preservation Alliance, Brenda Miller of the Hartford History Center of the Hartford Public Library, Richard C. Malley of the Connecticut Historical Society, Trix Rosen of Trix Rosen Photography Ltd., Reverend Dr. Edward Horstmann of Immanuel Congregational Church and Bill Uricchio of St. John's Episcopal Church.

CHAPTER ONE

VANISHING HARTFORD

*The former resident of Hartford, even though he may have been absent for a
decade, would on his return be surprised at the change in the business section, but
should he have been absent a generation he would be at first unacquainted with
his surroundings.*
*Such an one I discovered one pleasant Saturday afternoon in the summer,
standing on the corner of Main and Asylum streets, and looking about him in
a bewildered way. Elbowing my way through the crowd I put my hand on his
shoulder and called him by the "nick name" of our schoolboy days, when he
turned to me with the query, "Is this Hartford?"*

—Julius G. Rathbun, 1899[1]

It has been over a century since Julius G. Rathbun encountered his friend
on a Hartford street. In that time, the city changed even more drastically
than the two men could have imagined. Numerous buildings that would
have been familiar to them and were considered the pinnacle of size and
design have since vanished. Some have been replaced by other buildings.
Others are now parking lots that leave no immediately observable trace of
the architectural treasures that once stood there.

Hartford has had many notable structures over the years, dating back
to the seventeenth century. The oldest survivors today date from the late
eighteenth century. One of these is the Old State House. Built in 1796, it
served as statehouse, as city hall and, more recently, as a museum. Today,

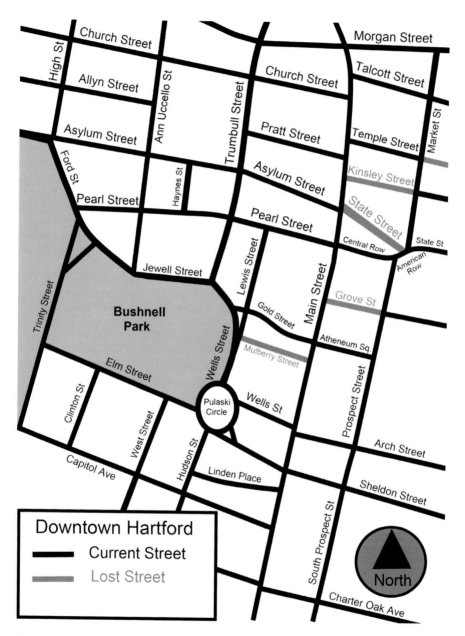

Map of area covered in the book. *Created by the author.*

much younger buildings surround it. These were all constructed at different times, and each of them replaced earlier structures that had once stood on the same spot. If it were possible to take snapshots of this area from each decade since the 1790s, we would see many different structures rise and fall here, some surviving longer than others, until we reached the current shape of the urban landscape. The same process could be applied to other adjacent areas of downtown Hartford. Each of the buildings that survive today is a reminder of a past period in the city's history. Buildings that have not survived were an important part of that history as well. They contributed to past cityscapes that residents and visitors navigated on a daily basis. By recalling these vanished environments, we recall something of the people who lived, worked and visited here.

The buildings themselves, both surviving and lost, were not static. Many of them have gone through different phases of growth and alteration to reach their later appearance. For instance, if we had looked at the Old State House in 1796, it would have lacked its distinctive cupola, which was added in 1827. If we had walked around the Old State House in 1860, we would have found a park-like area on its east side. There is a similar space there today, but from 1872 to 1934, we would have seen something else: a large and ornate federal building. Towering over the neighboring statehouse, it blocked the older building's front façade from view. Nor did this interloper on the statehouse grounds remain unchanged for all those years. In 1905, it was expanded for additional office space and lost one of its two distinctive towers. Looking at the area today, it is hard to imagine such a large building was here, and yet it was a feature of the cityscape that would have been instantly recognizable to the city's residents in that period.

It is also possible to imagine a time before the Old State House itself existed. It was preceded by a wood-frame building, built in 1720 and damaged by fire in 1783.

To know what Hartford's earliest lost buildings looked like, we have to rely on written descriptions, the occasional drawing and comparisons with similar structures that have survived to more recent times. There are many illustrations and photographs from the nineteenth century. They provide a record of individual buildings and entire streetscapes. By the turn of the twentieth century, an interest in preserving history had developed, and many places of note were photographed, often on the brink of their being lost forever.

In a densely built urban center like downtown Hartford, once one of the most prosperous cities in the nation, it is inevitable that larger buildings would have often replaced smaller ones. Expanding business, changing architectural tastes and modern urban renewal have all played a part in the rate and extent of change. Not every vanished building from the past could have been saved or even necessarily should have been saved, but by thinking about the great landmarks of Hartford's past, we can better reflect on what should be built in the future and which of today's historic treasures should not be lost.

A NINETEENTH-CENTURY SURVIVOR ON CENTRAL ROW AND ITS LOST NEIGHBORS

Many blocks in Hartford are the products of a gradual process of demolition and replacement. This sequence leaves a row consisting of various structures built at different times on the same block. If each old building on the block could share its memories, it would recall that it once had neighbors that have since passed away.

A good example of this is the four-story building at Six Central Row. Central Row faces the Old State House on its south side and has been home to many notable buildings from Hartford's earliest days. These included Hartford's second congregational meetinghouse of 1638. Number Six was built in 1850[2] and has a front of brownstone. Quarried down the Connecticut River in Portland, brownstone was used frequently on commercial buildings in the mid-nineteenth century. Number Six's original neighbor on the west, at the corner of Main Street, was a brick structure, called the Central Row Building. It was erected in the 1820s by Henry L. Ellsworth, who was developing real estate in downtown Hartford at that time. Mayor of Hartford in 1835 and the first commissioner of the U.S. Patent Office, Henry Leavitt Ellsworth was the son of Oliver Ellsworth, a drafter of the United States Constitution and third chief justice of the United States. The Central Row Building, which at one time was home to the Hartford Museum and the *Hartford Times* newspaper, was torn down in 1855 to make way for the Hungerford & Cone Building.[3] Like Number Six, this was a brownstone-fronted structure. It had stores on the first floor with offices above. Designed by Hartford architect Octavius J. Jordan, Hungerford & Cone was one of Hartford's most architecturally significant buildings of the time, with a bracketed cornice and three different window designs for each of the three upper floors.

The building was purchased by the Hartford Trust Company in 1869. It remained the trust's office until 1919, when the company merged with the

The Hungerford & Cone Building when it was occupied by the Hartford Trust Company. Six Central Row is on the left. *Pre-1920 postcard, courtesy of Tomas Nenortas.*

Connecticut Trust & Safe Deposit Company. It was demolished the following year to make way for the Hartford-Connecticut Trust Company Building, an eighteen-story skyscraper that still stands today. In an architectural nod to its brownstone companion, the 1920 tower has a limestone base that matches the height of Six Central Row. The earlier building, in turn, then had its first floor remodeled in granite to better reflect the style of its much taller neighbor.[1]

Just east of Number Six was a Universalist church, built in 1824. D.F. Robinson, who had earlier built Number Six, acquired the property in 1860. He constructed another four-story commercial building on the site, but this time he did not utilize the popular brownstone. His new building was called the Marble Block. It was only the second marble building in Hartford after the Phoenix Bank of 1817. On August 25, 1860, the *Hartford Courant* noted that "Robinson's marble building is to be a beautiful structure," but continued:

> *Our opinion, like that of the masses, is to the effect that Central Row would have looked still better had it been continued in brown stone. However, as*

15

we do not pay for the building perhaps it is none of our business, and as Mr. Robinson does, it is no more than fit that he be allowed to suit himself.

In addition to stores and offices, the Marble Block also had a public hall on the third floor, originally called Robinson's Hall and later Central Hall. The building was owned by the Robinson family until 1925, when it was purchased by Travelers Insurance Company.[5] The company replaced it with an office tower, completed in 1928.

This section of Central Row today reflects two layers of history: the 1850s and the 1920s. When Six Central Row was built, it joined two buildings on either side that dated to the 1820s: the Central Row Building and the Universalist church. This layer and those that preceded it have vanished. They were replaced by the Hungerford & Cone Block and the Marble Block, contemporaries of Number Six, both of which lasted into the 1920s. These were then replaced by the two office towers, which reflect the building boom of the 1920s. Many blocks in Hartford can be viewed in a similar way as representing different layers of history.

BETWEEN GOLD STREET AND MULBERRY STREET

In some cases of modern urban development, entire blocks of older buildings are removed and replaced with something much larger. These blocks today reveal nothing of what once stood there. The most famous instance of this is Constitution Plaza, built in the 1960s, which replaced a neighborhood on Hartford's east side. Another example is the block of Main Street between Mulberry and Gold Streets. If you look at a map of Hartford today, you will not be able to find Mulberry Street. In 1965, it was absorbed into the Bushnell Plaza Redevelopment Project.[6] That building complex now fills the area between Gold Street on the north, Main Street on the east and Wells Street on the south and west. Mulberry Street once passed through the center of this block, between Wells and Main.

A notable building once stood on the southwest corner of Main and Gold Streets. The City Hotel was originally a three-story building, erected by Daniel Wadsworth in 1816. According to one account, "The south part, from the sitting room, was an old building at that time occupied as a boarding house, and was roofed in with the new part on the north." From 1817 to

1819, this building was the original home of the Connecticut Asylum for the Education of Deaf and Dumb Persons, which is today the American School for the Deaf. The building then became Bennett's Hotel. It is mentioned in William Austin's classic story "Peter Rugg: The Missing Man" (1824). On September 4, 1824, during his return tour of America, the Marquis de Lafayette was entertained at the hotel. Later, when it was called the City Hotel, Charles Dickens was a guest.[7]

In 1870, the hotel was remolded according to new plans drawn by architect O.H. Easton. According to an article entitled "City Hotel Improvements," which appeared in the *Hartford Courant* on June 1, 1869:

> *The lower portion of the building will be thoroughly reconstructed, to accommodate four stores…An entire new front will be put in, constructed of pressed bricks with stone trimmings, the height of the present front being increased about fifteen feet—making four stories and basement. Not the least attractive feature of the improvements will appear in a handsome French roof.*

The altered building survived until 1913, when it was again radically transformed. Pasquale M. D'Esopo, a banker and developer, hired architect Isaac A. Allen Jr. to redesign the structure. It was raised to five stories, and the French mansard roof was removed. In 1914, D'Esopo constructed a theater in the rear for "high class vaudeville" and "photoplays" (silent movies). It was leased to Sylvester Z. Poli, the theater impresario, and was called the Poli Palace Theater. This was the vaudeville and movie magnate's second theater in Hartford; he had opened Poli's Theater a few blocks south on Main Street in 1903. A display of "hundreds of vari-colored electric bulbs" decorated the exterior of the D'Esopo Building to celebrate the new theater's opening on May 25, 1914.[8]

D'Esopo also acquired the buildings just to the south of his building at Main and Gold Streets. He rebuilt them to connect to the rest of his building and match its architecture. Completed in 1916, the D'Esopo Building now extended the entire block, from Gold Street to Mulberry Street. In addition to twelve stores on the first floor and the Poli Palace Theater, the building contained two hundred office rooms, which made it "the second largest commercial public office building in the state" and "the largest and most valuable individual holding on Main street," according to the *Hartford Courant*. The paper further described it:

Hotel Heublein. The 1891 hotel is on the left. On the right is the original Heublein Building and Mulberry Street. *1908 postcard, courtesy of Tomas Nenortas.*

The style of architecture is French Renaissance with tapestry bricks and limestone trimmings and an ornamental cornice. New features in the form of polished granite, beveled glass and art glass windows have been used in decorating the store fronts.[9]

The theater was later known as the Loew-Poli Palace and the whole structure as the Palace Building. A product of the success of two Italian immigrants, D'Esopo and Poli, the building and theater were lost to the Bushnell Plaza redevelopment in 1964.

Also lost due to the project were the buildings a block west, which faced Bushnell Park across Wells Street. In 1859, Andrew Heublein opened his café and hotel in a four-story building at the southeast corner of Mulberry and Wells Streets. It was one of several businesses run by German immigrants that clustered on Mulberry Street in the nineteenth century.[10] After Heublein's death in 1875, his sons, Gilbert and Louis, continued the business under the name G.F. Heublein & Bro. From 1890 to 1891, they constructed a new hotel, attached to their father's original building, at the corner of Wells and Gold Streets. The new Hotel Heublein was an impressive five-story Romanesque building with a mansard roof and a corner tower. A March 3, 1891 article in the *Courant* admired "Hartford's New Hotel":

As the building progressed the exterior gave promise that the hotel was to be
a pretty if small one, but few, except those who have had glimpses of the
inside from time to time, were prepared for the careful regard for creature
comfort and artistic effect that has guided the interior treatment. Hard wood
wainscoting, floors and furniture, lace and plush curtains, the tiled floor
of the lobby, soft rugs, open fire-places and be-jewelled [sic] chandeliers
gladden the eye and give an air of luxury to the house.

In 1900, the hotel opened a roof-top garden and installed a long-distance telephone in each room for guests, which few hotels in the country had yet done.[11] Initially, G.F. Heublein personally managed the hotel, but he later entrusted its management to others. G.F. Heublein & Bro. was also a successful liquor and wine company that created the world's first bottled cocktails in 1892 and brought A1 Steak Sauce to the United States in 1895. The hotel survived under various managers until it was finally razed for the new development.

STATE STREET AND AMERICAN ROW

Returning to the area of the Old State House, there is another modern complex that occupies an entire block. State House Square, built in 1987, faces the Old State House from across a pedestrian-only area that was once the continuation of State Street. Before the major changes of the second half of the twentieth century, State Street ran east from Main Street to the Connecticut River. The section of State Street located north of the Old State House grounds, like Central Row to the south, had a long history of development and change. A surviving trace of this past is the historic façade of a building that was incorporated into the new complex. Built in 1899, it was designed by Ernest Flagg for the First National Bank. Many other notable buildings once existed on this block.

The northeast corner of Main and State Streets was long known as Exchange Corner, an indication of its importance as a center of commerce. The corner building was destroyed in a fire in 1832, but it was rebuilt and survived into the twentieth century. In 1899, Julius Rathbun noted that

the interior arrangement of Exchange Block remains practically as of
old. The entrances and stairways narrow and dark, the offices with low

ceilings, the stairs well worn by the footsteps of many thousands who have climbed them.[12]

In 1927, the Harvey & Lewis Building, an eight-story art deco tower, was completed on the corner of Main and State Streets. Foster E. Harvey and Robert H. Lewis were opticians, and their company is still in business today. The building was demolished in 1984, to make way for the construction of State House Square. In the nineteenth century, several doors east from Exchange Corner, was a building that housed the United States Hotel. For decades, this was one of Hartford's premier hotels, where many businessmen and politicians stayed when they were in the city, as well as baseball players when Hartford was in the National League. Until a new statehouse was built in the 1870s, the hotel was the headquarters of the Republican Party during political conventions and sessions of the general assembly. The hotel began under the management of Jabez Ripley and was taken over by Homer Morgan in 1829. By the early 1840s, it was managed by S.G. Boughton, and in the 1850s, it was taken over by Harvey Rockwood. In 1855, Rockwood added a four-story addition to the hotel. In 1859 came another new feature: "A handsome entrance to the main hall of the Hotel, surmounted by a balcony, entered from the upper hall."[13] In 1865, David A. Rood took over management of the United States Hotel. He would not completely retire from running the hotel until 1899.

East of the United States Hotel was the Eagle Hotel, first run by Edson Fessenden in the 1830s, who had an interest in a stage line. In 1851, prior to taking over the United States Hotel, David Rood became the manager of the Eagle Hotel. In 1855, he enlarged the hotel with a five-story addition to the rear. He also renamed the establishment the "Trumbull House," a change that the *Courant* praised on November 27, 1855: "The old Eagle Hotel was a good house in its day, but the name did not quite indicate the real rank of the house," whereas the new name "is just the thing for a first class hotel in Connecticut." He bought the Trumbull House in 1867, and in 1869, he consolidated it with the United States Hotel, which came to be, for many years, the largest hotel in the state.[14] As described in the *Courant*: "While both hotels were entirely distinct under the old management, they are now as closely nitted [*sic*] and have as convenient accommodations by stairways, halls, and entrances, as if originally erected to go together."[15]

The east section of the lower floor of the Trumbull House was leased for commercial use. It came to be occupied by the First National Bank, which later acquired the rest of the property. In 1899, the bank constructed its

State Street, circa 1900. *From right to left*: the Hartford National Bank, the First National Bank (formerly the Eagle Hotel), the United States Hotel (with balcony above the main entrance) and other buildings ending at Exchange Corner. *Hartford Collection, Hartford History Center, Hartford Public Library*.

building, which is now part of State House Square. That same year, Rood finally retired at the age of eighty-two and filed for bankruptcy. According to the *Courant*, Rood said that

> *his failure was to be attributed to the falling off in business, caused in part by the fact that customers were patronizing the newer hotels which had all the modern improvements...Mr. Rood spoke of the admirable site of the States for a modern hotel and said that if it had been torn down years ago and a modern hotel erected on the site, it would have retained its prestige as the leading commercial house in the city, which it held for many years.*[16]

The United States Hotel was kept open by the owner of the property, James J. Goodwin, until 1901, when it was converted into offices. It was eventually torn down in 1924 for a new store erected by the W.T. Grant Company.

Next to the Eagle Hotel/Trumbull House was the longtime home of the Hartford National Bank, which resembled an ancient Greek temple. It was described in an 1892 history of the bank:

October 26, 1811, the bank moved into its present quarters on State Street. For Grecian symmetry and obvious adaptation to uses required, the edifice, after the lapse of eighty years, in the presence of imposing architecture of recent date, still remains one of the most attractive in the city. The dome over the front room was added about the year 1820, and as a work of art both in form and decoration, bears the closest study. [17]

In 1912, when the bank was on the verge of moving into a new skyscraper at the corner of Main and Asylum Streets, the *Courant* noted that

it is like walking backwards a hundred years to go from the State street [side]walk into the upper back room of the bank, with antiquated paper on the walls and the secret cupboard in which the ledgers were hidden for so many years. In these old chambers, once the sleeping rooms of clerks at night as they kept guard over their treasure, they tapped on the wall one day five or six years ago and found hidden therein 125 volumes of the bank's past records, and there was no one living who knew how or when the shelves were boarded and papered over. A stock certificate, hidden in one of the books, was delivered to its proper owner after 100 years delay. [18]

No sooner had the bank vacated its historic State Street premises than the venerable building was torn down to make way for a new vaudeville house called the Princess Theater. [19]

Next to the bank, on the east, stood the 1880 Hartford Courant Building, designed by architect George Keller. Next to that was the Exchange Bank, which had been established in 1834. The bank added a new brownstone front in 1869. Designed by Bryant & Rogers of Boston, it featured Corinthian columns and pilasters. After the bank merged with the First National Bank in 1916, the building was purchased by John C. Long and Timothy J. Long, who owned Long's Hotel next door. They leased the former bank building to run a Chinese restaurant. [20]

Long's Hotel was located in the Gregory Building, constructed in 1871. On January 1, 1895, the Long brothers took possession of the building, where they operated a restaurant. They converted it into a hotel and soon expanded into adjoining properties on State and Market Streets. John Long was a regular competitor in the Highland Games and had won prizes in the caber toss. His hotel soon became popular with other athletes. The Longs also had a very successful catering business. After the brothers retired in 1921, Long's became the Hotel Oxford. The building was torn down in 1936. [21]

Just to the southeast of the Old State House is the famous elliptical building, constructed in 1963 for Phoenix Mutual Life Insurance Company. Its address is One American Row, a street that was named for another of Hartford's great hostelries, the American Hotel. The origins of this institution are vague, but a hotel existed on the corner of State Street and American Row from the early nineteenth century. By the mid-nineteenth century, the building consisted of two sections, north and south. The north section was the American Hotel while the south section contained American Hall, used for theatrical entertainments, balls and dances. Part of the south section was removed when the Parsons' Theater was built on Prospect Street in 1896. For four decades, the grandly ornate Parsons was Hartford's leading theater. Many productions premiered there before their debuts on Broadway.[22] According to one contemporary description:

> *All the first-class musical and dramatic productions playing* [in] *New England are booked at Parsons' Theatre, one of the very best of the high-class theatres in the eastern states and playing only the attractions that the "big cities" get...H.C. Parsons, manager of the theatre which bears his name, is a manager of long years' standing. He has made his house one of the best on the eastern circuit, and attracts people to his house because of its beauty, its convenience of locality and the excellent management under which it is directed...The play house is beautifully decorated, a feature in itself that has made it inviting and attractive, and added much to its financial success.*[23]

The American Hotel was torn down in 1925 and Parsons' Theater in 1936.

THE PHOENIX NATIONAL BANK

The block of Main Street across from the Old State House has been home to a number of the city's most important buildings. For almost a century and a half, the Phoenix Bank, as it was originally called, had a prominent place among them. Between 1815 and 1964, there were four different versions of the bank. They reflected the growth of the bank and the different types of architecture that found favor over the years.

The Phoenix Bank was incorporated in 1814 and reorganized as the Phoenix National Bank in 1865. The first bank in Hartford not controlled by

The first Phoenix National Bank Building (1815), Main Street. The two lion sculptures can be seen above the wings to the right and left. *Taylor Collection, State Archives, Connecticut State Library.*

Congregationalists, it was originally dubbed the "Episcopal Bank." Its initial home was in the Main Street house of Thomas Olcott, an original director of the bank. The house was later destroyed by fire. The bank then erected its first building in 1815 on land donated by Olcott and his two unmarried sisters.[21] It was Hartford's first marble structure, and its classical-inspired design reflected the popularity of the Federal style of architecture in the early republic. According to a history of the bank:

> *The office floor was above a basement and was reached by flights of iron-railed steps at each end of a spacious platform, itself, by its location and accessibility, to be one of the features of Hartford. A figure of the phoenix bird, carved in wood, surmounted the [façade]. It was on this platform that Commodore McDonough, the hero of the recent war [of 1812], stood in February, 1817, when he received the beautiful sword given by Hartford citizens and now preserved by the Connecticut Historical Society. Also it was from this platform that some of the dignitaries witnessed the parade on the occasion of Lafayette's visit, September 3, 1824, the general himself standing under an arch which spanned the street at this point.*[25]

In 1827, two wings were added on either side of the bank and were rented for shops. The wooden phoenix was replaced by one carved in stone, and two life-sized marble lions were placed above each of the wings. The bank had used only sixty feet of its one-hundred-foot lot for the building, so the remaining forty feet were sold. They were later used for the construction of a four-story brownstone building, erected by William H. Imlay in 1850.[26] The building's main tenant was the State Bank, which had been incorporated in 1849.

The first Phoenix Bank Building was replaced by a new one in 1873–74. A building of four stories above a raised basement, it was designed in a French Second Empire style by Hartford architect George Keller. The contractor was James G. Batterson. As with the previous building, the entrance was above street level and reached by a flight of stairs. Stairs on either side of the front entrance led to shops in the basement level. The phoenix sculpture from the first building was reused on the newer and taller structure. The lions, which had adorned the two wings of the previous building, were now brought down to street level to stand guard on either side of the bank's new façade. In an article on "The Phoenix Bank Building," on May 24, 1873, the *Hartford Courant* described the building soon to be constructed:

Main Street, circa 1901. *From left to right*: the Connecticut Mutual Life Insurance Company Building (as expanded in 1901), the State Bank (1850), the second Phoenix National Bank Building (1874) and the Corning Building (1874). *Hartford Collection, Hartford History Center, Hartford Public Library.*

Opposite: The third Phoenix Bank Building (1906), Main Street. *Taylor Collection, State Archives, Connecticut State Library.*

> *The entrance is approached by a short flight of granite steps and is boldly projected from the face of the building—on each side are two polished gray granite columns supporting an entablature...The basement is to be of granite, and the rest of the façade is intended to be of white marble.*

By 1905, the bank required larger quarters. The old building was expanded with a new façade of five stories and a rear addition. The new front was more modern in appearance, being flatter and more box like than its predecessor. The entrance was moved to street level, in keeping with the times and the demand for greater convenience and accessibility. As the *Courant* noted, "Modern banking methods require that the bank shall be closer to

the people, on a grade with the street, so that people can do business quickly and get out."[27] It should be noted that businesses often rented space in their office buildings to other companies. For instance, when the new building opened in 1906, the Phoenix National Bank occupied the south side of the first floor, while the American National Bank occupied the north side.[28]

The stone phoenix was again placed atop the new building. The lions retained their places on the sidewalk throughout the construction. In 1912, city authorities decided that the lions encroached on the street line and ordered that they be removed. The bank complied, "though loud were the protests from lovers of art and from citizens who as boys had patted, bestraddled and helped polish those lions, even as the street urchins of the twentieth century were wont to do."[29] As the *Hartford Courant* related,

Many of the youth of Hartford have been entertained by fond papas with stories about the lions and the things they did when everybody was asleep and nobody was around to keep tabs on them.[30]

The bank presented the lions to the city for use at the new Municipal Building. They can be seen there today, guarding the entrance on the Arch Street side of the building.

In 1907–8, the State Bank, which adjoined the Phoenix Bank on the south, also constructed a new building. Designed by Benjamin Wistar Morris, its façade was dominated by a large vaulted opening around the entrance, which resembled a triumphal arch. This motif was popular in the classically influenced bank architecture of the time.[31] Within this opening was the entrance to the bank, which had solid bronze doors. The *Courant* praised the new building extravagantly, calling it "the most complete building in the country devoted exclusively to the business of banking."[32]

By the 1920s, the Phoenix National Bank was again in need of additional space. Remodeling the interior of its existing building was discovered to be as expensive as building a new one, so the bank decided to build again from scratch. The fourth and final Phoenix National Bank Building was a nine-story structure built in 1923–24. The architects were Dennison & Hirons of New York and the general contractors were Marc Eidlitz & Son. Its exterior was of Indiana limestone with a base of granite. Like the State Bank, it incorporated a large vaulted area above the entrance, which had an ornamental grille inspired by the works of the Spanish masters. The top of the building had a new sculpture of a phoenix. The stonework on the lower levels of the building was clearly a nod to the architecture of the original

Main Street. *From left to right*: the State Bank (1908), the Fourth Phoenix National Bank Building (1924) and the Corning Building (1930). *Stockel Collection, Hartford History Center, Hartford Public Library.*

Phoenix Bank of 1815. The new building was opened for inspection by visitors on June 9, 1924. The *Courant* reported that 17,934 people came and were enthusiastic in their praise.[33]

Both the Phoenix National Bank and the State Bank later merged with other institutions. Both buildings were demolished in 1964 to make way for the new Hartford National Bank Building.

CHAPTER TWO

TRAVELERS AND AETNA INSURANCE COMPANIES

Hartford is famous for insurance. The large buildings of Travelers Insurance on Main Street and Aetna Insurance on Farmington Avenue are testaments to the importance of this industry. Before these two companies moved to their current headquarters in the early twentieth century, they had various homes. For a number of years, Travelers was located on Prospect Street. The company then moved to Main Street, where it constructed its current building on the block between Grove Street (which no longer extends to Main Street) and Atheneum Square. The Travelers complex replaced a number of earlier buildings there, including one of the longtime homes of Aetna.

TRAVELERS ON PROSPECT STREET

The Travelers Insurance Company was founded by James G. Batterson in 1864. According to a souvenir booklet that visitors received upon the opening of the company's new building in 1913,

> *Mr. Batterson's attention was first called to the subject of accident insurance while traveling in England in 1859, when he purchased at Leamington an insurance ticket issued by the Railway Passengers Assurance Society of London, insuring the traveler in case of accidental death or injury while*

Travelers Insurance Company Building, corner of Prospect and Grove Streets, 1907. *Library of Congress, Prints & Photographs Division, Detroit Publishing Company Collection.*

traveling from Leamington to Liverpool. It was this ticket which first suggested to him the possibilities of a business providing insurance against accidents of all kinds.[34]

The company began business in two rooms on the second floor of a building at the southeast corner of Main and Kinsley Streets. Within a few months, it moved to larger quarters in a building at the corner of Asylum Street and Union Place, facing the railroad station. When Travelers moved a third time, to Prospect Street in 1872, the *Hartford Courant* speculated that

the removal of the large and familiar sign of the "Travelers Insurance Company," which has so long conspicuously faced the depot, will leave many railroad travelers in doubt as to whether they have really arrived in Hartford.[35]

Travelers moved to the Ellsworth House, built by Henry L. Ellsworth in the early 1820s.[36] The company made numerous additions and renovations to the house until it grew into a substantial structure. The company also erected a printing building in 1903 and a supply and storage building in 1905. By this time, "it became evident that the old Home Office had reached the limit of expansion and a much larger and more modern building was imperatively demanded." Travelers decided to construct a new home office on Main Street. In 1905, it acquired land on the northeast corner of Main and Grove Streets and soon built the first section of new building.[37] Travelers' old building on Prospect Street was acquired by the Hartford Steam Boiler Inspection & Insurance Company in 1907. That company replaced it with a new art deco building in 1932.

TRAVELERS ON MAIN STREET

The Travelers Building we know today was constructed in three major sections. The corner stone of the first section, at Main and Grove Streets, was laid on June 29, 1906, and the building was occupied on May 7, 1907. Two buildings along Main Street were removed to construct this section, the Putnam Building and the Hartford City Gas Light Company.

The Putnam Building had stood on the corner. It had originally been a house designed by Henry Austin of New Haven. It was built in 1848 for Asa Farwell, a successful liquor dealer with a business on Commerce Street. According to an article on "The Old Putnam Building" that appeared in the *Courant* on March 12, 1901:

> *It was considered one of the finest private houses in town and was pointed out with pride to visitors to the city. The bricks of which it was made were brought from Philadelphia by water. They were the genuine article and experts in masonry say that there are no finer bricks in Hartford to-day. Mr. Farwell was famous for his cherry bounce and it was said that the profit on one glass of this popular beverage paid for one of the bricks in the house.*

After Farwell's death the house was used as offices by various companies, including the Putnam Fire Insurance Company, from which the building

Main Street, 1905. *From left to right*: The Putnam Building (1848), the Hartford City Gas Light Company Building (1894) and the Unitarian Church's 1899 commercial building. *Thompson Photographs of Hartford, State Archives, Connecticut State Library.*

took its name. The Putnam Building was much altered before it was finally torn down for the Travelers Building.

Next door to the Putnam Building had been the three-story Hartford City Gas Light Company Building. Built in 1894, it was a particularly ornate Renaissance revival structure designed by George Keller. Its construction replaced an old house on the site. It had been built in 1806 by the father of Thomas H. Gallaudet, the famed educator of the deaf. In 1829, the house was acquired by Ezra Clark and remained in the Clark family until it was sold to the Hartford City Gas Light Company in 1893.

The 1906 section of Travelers was only part of what the company planned to eventually build. Its next step was related in the 1913 booklet:

The plans adopted for the Home Office of the Travelers provided for a building of which the part completed in May, 1907, was but little more than half. It was computed at that time that at the ratio of growth then prevailing it would be seven years before it was necessary to complete the building; but the growth of the Company has been more rapid, so that it was necessary to commence the addition at the end of five years. April 1ˢᵗ, 1912, the demolition of the old building on the site of the extension was commenced, and the fiftieth anniversary of the company finds the entire building completed, including the erection of the new part and the remodeling of the old.[38]

The extension was erected in 1912–13 on an area that had recently belonged to the Universalist Church of the Redeemer. The demolished buildings included the church itself and a commercial building that stood in front of it on Main Street. Before the church was built in 1860, the property was the site of the Chenevard House. For nearly fifty years the house, built around 1724, had been the well-known Black Horse Tavern.[39]

The third section of Travelers, the 527-foot office tower, was built to the east of the earlier sections. Travelers Tower was the tallest building in New England when it was completed in 1919. Designed by Donn Barber, the Travelers Building continues today as one of Hartford's great architectural monuments.

AETNA ON MAIN STREET

Aetna was founded as a fire insurance company in 1819. The company organized a life insurance department in 1850, which was incorporated as a separate company in 1853. For many years, both of these companies had headquarters in the block south of the Travelers Building. In the mid-nineteenth century, two houses stood just south of the Universalist Church property: the Conklin House and the Hendee House. In 1867, the Aetna Insurance Company constructed a mansard-roofed brownstone building on the Hendee property. This would remain its headquarters until 1903. In that year, work began on a new building that replaced the 1867 building and the neighboring Conklin House.[40] Designed by Benjamin Wistar Morris, it was a five-story structure with a highly ornamented Neoclassical façade. According to a description of the prospective development in an article, "Aetna's New Building," that appeared in the *Hartford Courant* on June 29, 1903:

The design of the façade is extremely simple in its general composition, but it is thought will be very impressive on account of the large scale of

The 1867 Aetna (Fire) Insurance Company Building, Main Street. On the left is the Conklin House. *The Memorial History of Hartford County.*

its component parts. For instance, the three-quarter engaged Corinthian columns are four feet in diameter and 36 feet high or a third larger than those of the Center Church and three feet higher than the New York Public Library columns, and as their bases will be twenty feet or more above the sidewalk the effect will be impressive.

There were construction delays due to a particularly harsh winter in 1903–04 and a fire in a Rochester, New York factory that consumed the mahogany woodwork intended for the building's interior. The building was eventually completed in 1905.[11]

Between the Aetna (Fire) Building and Atheneum Square were the Phillips and Toucey properties. The Phillips Building was originally built for the publishing firm of Hudson & Goodwin. In 1796, this company published *American Cookery*, by Amelia Simmons, the first cookbook written by an American. They also published the *Hartford Courant* there from 1796 to 1815.[12] The neighboring Toucey House was built in the first decade of the nineteenth century by Chauncey Gleason, a dry goods merchant. It was then owned by Cyprian Nichols, whose daughter Catherine married Isaac Toucey in 1827. Toucey (1792–1868) served as governor of Connecticut (1846–47), attorney general of the United States in the administration of James K. Polk and secretary of the navy in the administration of James Buchanan.

The Phillips and Toucey Buildings were demolished in 1868 to make way for the new building of the Charter Oak Life Insurance Company.[13] Built in 1869–70, the building was designed by the prominent Boston architectural firm of Bryant & Rogers. The six-story structure was one of the most impressive in Hartford at the time:

The street façades are to be faced with the elegant material of which the Boston City Hall and Horticultural Hall are constructed, the same being obtained from the quarry of the Granite Railway company in Concord, N.H...Both elevations are designed in the French Renaissance style, with details believed to be more ornate than heretofore introduced into the street edifices of our principal cities.[14]

In 1888, the Charter Oak Life Insurance Company ended operations and the building became the home of the Aetna Life Insurance Company. In 1912–14, the company dramatically altered the building by adding four stories and replacing the original mansard roof with a much flatter roof. The project, to plans by Donn Barber, required a significant feat of engineering:

The construction of the additional floors above the original building is of such a nature that no weight rests upon the foundation of the original building, the weight of the addition resting upon eight concrete and steel piers.[15]

Aetna Life completed its massive new home office on Farmington Avenue in 1931. The old building was rented out until the Aetna (Fire) Insurance Company purchased it in 1939. From that time, Aetna owned both of the buildings just south of the Travelers Building. In 1957, Travelers purchased the two buildings from Aetna, thus extending its property to Atheneum Square. In 1963, Travelers demolished both buildings to make way for a grand entrance plaza on the south side of the Travelers Tower.

CHAPTER THREE

PEARL STREET

The "Wall Street of Hartford"

Beginning at Main Street, just southwest of the Old State House, Pearl Street runs westward, intersecting with Trumbull and Ann Uccello Streets before it ends at Ford Street, across from Bushnell Park. The street dates back to Hartford's earliest colonial days, when it began as a path from the meetinghouse to Matthew Allyn's Mill on the Little River (later called the Park River).[46] By the mid-nineteenth century, Pearl Street was lined with a number of residences and small businesses. Also located on the street was a printing company and, at its western end, the county jail. By the early twentieth century, Pearl Street had developed into a prominent business thoroughfare, home to the headquarters of several important banks and insurance companies. A *Hartford Courant* article in 1921 noted that in financial circles, Pearl Street was becoming known as the "Wall Street of Hartford."[47] Today, most of those earlier structures have made way for much larger buildings, many of which have their main façades facing Main or Trumbull Streets. Recalling Pearl Street in earlier days, however, reminds us of notable examples of urban architecture that were once found on what was then one of the city's most bustling streets.

The eastern end of Pearl Street is today flanked by two modern office towers that face Main Street. At the southwestern corner of Main and Pearl is One Financial Plaza, popularly called the Gold Building, a twenty-six-floor structure completed in 1974. On the other corner of Pearl Street, at 777 Main Street, is another building with twenty-six floors, built by the Hartford National Bank between 1964 and 1967.

Looking east on Pearl Street. *Circa 1920s postcard, courtesy of Tomas Nenortas.*

UNION HALL AND THE CONNECTICUT MUTUAL LIFE INSURANCE COMPANY

The northwest corner of Main and Pearl has had an interesting history. A sixteenth-century residence, built by Thomas Olcott, occupied the property until 1826. In that year, the land was leased to Nathan Allyn, who tore down the old house and in the following year erected a three-story brick building. One of the more substantial structures in the city at the time, it had a large public assembly hall on the third floor with various offices and shops below. It was originally called Allyn's Hall, but when Mr. Allyn failed financially in 1838, the building was acquired by William H. Imlay, whose own fine residence stood just to the west on Pearl Street. Allyn was a Democrat and Allyn's Hall had gained a reputation as a gathering place for members of the Democratic Party. Imlay, the new owner, was a member of the Whig Party. To end the association of his new building with Allyn and the Democrats, Imlay grandly renamed it Union Hall. In 1867, Union Hall was bought by the Connecticut Mutual Life Insurance Company, which constructed its own grand building on the site in 1870–72. This was not the end for Union Hall, however. The old building was acquired by Erastus Smith, Esq., and moved to the corner of Farmington Avenue and Flower Street, where it was rebuilt. For many years thereafter, it was known as the Union Hall Hotel and later as the Farmington Avenue Hotel.[18]

The building that replaced Union Hall on the corner of Main and Pearl became one of the greatest architectural treasures in Hartford's history. Towering over its neighbors of the 1870s, the Connecticut Mutual Building was intended to be a monument that would rank with any of the other prominent structures recently erected by life insurance companies in other major cities. The building was designed by the architects Gridley J.F. Bryant and Louis P. Rogers, the former being one of the most important architects of Victorian-era Boston. Reflecting the inspiration of the French Second Empire style, the four main floors of the Connecticut Mutual Building's highly detailed granite façade featured columns and pilasters, with a two-story portico above the front entrance that was enhanced by statuary. Dentil moldings ran along the building's prominent cornice, above which were a hip roof with elaborate dormers and a mansard-roofed tower on each of the four corners. The contract for the stonework was awarded to James G. Batterson, Hartford's nationally renowned granite supplier and builder.[19]

Although this distinctive building would survive until the construction of the Hartford National Bank Building in the 1960s, it would undergo a number of changes over the years that gradually diminished its original architectural impact. In 1900, the company approved plans for a massive expansion. Having recently acquired the adjacent property to the west along Pearl Street, the company decided to construct a new building there of eight stories, connected on each floor to the earlier building on the inside. The architect for the new construction was Ernest Flagg, who had recently designed the First National Bank on State Street. So that the old structure would match the height of the new, it was raised two stories, necessitating the removal of the hip roof and four towers. The changes did not end there. The front entrance on Main Street, formerly reached by ascending a broad flight of stairs, was moved to street level. This alteration required that much of the heavy stonework making up the two-level portico above the entrance also be removed, including a symbolic statuary group depicting a widow and orphan receiving their just rights from the cornucopia of plenty.[50]

Excavations for the new building on the former site of the Pearl Street Congregational Church resulted in the interesting discovery of an old well, "thirty feet deep and finely set about with large stones." The well, uncovered "at about the southeast corner of the base of the old tower of the church," belonged to the residence of William H. Imlay, whose home had occupied the property before the church was built.[51] The excavations also resulted in some innovation for Hartford. The contractor, Edward Balf, decided to make use of "a 25-horse power engine and boom derrick with six tubes from which the carts will be loaded," marking "the first time that a boom derrick was ever used for an excavation of this character in this city."[52]

Space in the new structure was allocated to the Connecticut Trust & Safe Deposit Company, a tenant of the front section of the old building, who would lose space due to the changes being made. Connecticut Mutual had high hopes that the new building would attract many new tenants with its central location and a square footage that made it the largest structure of its kind in the city at that time.[53] In April 1902, the first tenants to move in to the completed building were the Mechanics Savings Bank, Ward W. Jacobs's railroad and steamship ticket agency and the office of Cedar Hill Cemetery.[54] By 1903, they were joined by the Scottish Union & National Fire Insurance Company and the Aetna (Fire) Insurance Company, whose new building on Main Street was being built at the time. The building was described as being "unquestionably the finest between New York and Boston and is the equal of the finest in those great cities."[55]

The Connecticut Mutual Life Insurance Company continued to occupy its newly expanded quarters for almost a quarter century until 1925, when it sold its property at Pearl and Main Streets to the United States Security

Trust Company. The new owners merged with the Hartford-Aetna National Bank in 1927 to form the Hartford National Bank and Trust Company. The new bank decided to make more alterations to the old 1870 building, which had already been "shorn of its mansard top-gear as well as its front trimmings," almost thirty years earlier.[56] In 1928, the first two floors were combined and redesigned to accommodate a massive new half-acre banking space. The exterior of the first two floors was also completely transformed, the old exterior columns being replaced with large granite piers to create a modern look. The last of the façade statuary was also removed.[57] Thus drastically simplified, the building would survive until the bank finally demolished it for good in 1964. The 1902 building would survive just a little longer, brought down in 1966 to make way for a two-story extension at the back of the new office tower.[58]

THE STATE SAVINGS BANK AND THE FIRE DEPARTMENT

To the south across the street from the Connecticut Mutual properties was a three-story brownstone building at Thirty-nine Pearl Street. Built in 1853 by the Hartford Life & Health Insurance Company, it was typical of the many Italianate-styled business blocks constructed in the city in the mid-nineteenth century. The company, founded in 1849, was at one time "considered one of the strongest in the city" but soon ran into serious trouble, as related in the *Memorial History of Hartford County*:

> *Its disastrous health business, and a very singular and illegitimate speculation which was really property insurance, and utterly foreign to the true object of life insurance,—the insuring of negro slaves for their masters, and of shiploads of coolies in transit to South America, Cuba, etc.,—fatally weakened it, and a fierce quarrel among the directorate helped to discredit it outside. Its days being evidently numbered the president and secretary and Chester Adams (director and sheriff) bought out the other stockholders and wound up the company, finishing in 1859.[59]*

Adams would be the first president of the new State Savings Bank, which began to rent rooms at Thirty-nine Pearl Street and eventually bought the building in 1869. The bank placed a gilded sculpture over the front entrance

The State Savings Bank, Pearl Street. To the right is the Phoenix Mutual Life Insurance Company Building. *Taylor Collection, State Archives, Connecticut State Library.*

depicting a beehive with two cornucopias overflowing with gold coins, symbolizing the rewards of saving money.[60]

A driveway to the right of the bank led to a smaller building behind it with the address of Forty-three Pearl Street. For many years, this was the headquarters of Hartford's fire department, which was officially established in 1864. It purchased a fire bell in 1867 and built a tower in which to hang it behind its headquarters. The department moved to a new headquarters, built farther west on Pearl Street in 1918–19, but the old building continued to be used by Chemical Engine Company Number Nine (renamed Squad A in 1910) until 1921. In that year, the State Savings Bank acquired the building. The old fire bell was taken down, to the disappointment of the many citizens who were used to setting their watches to its ringing twice a day, at noon and 6:00 p.m. The bell is now in the collections of the Connecticut Historical Society.[61]

On June 12, 1921, with the fire station's days numbered, the *Hartford Courant* printed a story entitled, "Squad A House Has Farewell Party," noting that *in a few days the doors of the old house will open for the last time, the old walls will give a final answering tremble to the rumble of heavy wheels, the stone-flagged driveway will be alive once more with the glitter of red enamel and polished brass, the clang of gongs and the shouts of men, and then the old house will become quiet, living only in the memories of those who, for a few fleeting years, served under the shadow of its historic bell-tower.*

The State Savings Bank had moved out of its Pearl Street building in 1914 and took up quarters in the Phoenix Bank Building on Main Street. In 1921, it reacquired its old headquarters and the old fire station but the following year replaced them with a new building, which continued to have the earlier address of Thirty-nine Pearl Street. Having elected not to construct a large office building, the bank instead erected a smaller but graceful Colonial revival banking house. Designed by Benjamin Wistar Morris, it had a Greek temple front with triangular pediment and columns. The bank later built a rear two-story addition in the area of the old firehouse.[62] In 1968, the State Savings Bank merged with the Dime Savings Bank to form the State Dime Savings Bank. The building was eventually demolished in the early 1970s to make way for the development of One Financial Plaza (the Gold Building).

NATIONAL FIRE INSURANCE COMPANY

Before the demolitions of the 1970s, the south side of Pearl Street from the State Savings Bank to Trumbull Street displayed the architectural products of two building booms, one in the 1890s and the other in the 1920s. Until the late nineteenth century, this section of Pearl had been home to a number of low-rise blocks with shops on their ground floors. Hartford's continued development as an insurance and banking center made it inevitable that more and more of these modest buildings would be replaced by the most up-to-date office buildings.

The Brinley House, on the southwest corner of Pearl and Lewis Streets, was demolished to make way for the new building of the National Fire Insurance Company at Ninety-five Pearl Street. Organized in 1871, National Fire was a successor to the earlier Merchants' Insurance Company, which had been forced to liquidate due to heavy claims from the great Chicago fire of that year. The National occupied offices in the Charter Oak Bank Building, at the corner of Asylum and Trumbull Streets, before moving into

National Fire Insurance Company Building, Pearl Street. *Circa 1911 postcard, courtesy of Tomas Nenortas.*

its new headquarters on Pearl Street in 1893. Designed by Hartford architect William C. Brocklesby in the style of the Italian Renaissance, the building's three elaborately detailed stories above a high basement displayed the use of pink granite, Longmeadow brownstone, Roman brick and terra cotta. "The general expression of the exterior of the building is that of dignity, elegance and repose," stated the *Hartford Courant*, which noted that it "combines with its modest beauty a thorough adaptability for every-day work."[63]

National Fire remained on Pearl Street until it moved to a new building on Asylum Avenue in 1941. Its old home was occupied from 1945 to the early 1960s by offices of the Veterans' Administration. The current office building on the site was constructed in 1970–71 by the United Bank and Trust Company.

PHOENIX MUTUAL LIFE INSURANCE COMPANY

Another insurance company to build on Pearl Street in the 1890s was Phoenix Mutual Life. This business was established in 1851 as the American Temperance Life Insurance Company, which provided discounted policies to those who abstained from alcohol. The company's plan did not work out:

> *Solicitors found the restrictions placed upon the freedom of the individual an ever-present obstacle, blocking the persuasive force of their eloquence. Satisfied after a fair trial that, however correct the principle might be, the attempted application of it ran counter to the inclinations of human nature, the managers abandoned the temperance feature in 1861, conformed the rates and contracts to the common practice, and with legislative permission changed the name to the Phoenix Mutual Life Insurance Company.*[64]

The company built its headquarters at Forty-nine Pearl Street in 1896–97 on the site of the old Tertius Wadsworth estate (Wadsworth had been the company's first vice-president). Like the National Fire Building, it was designed in the style of the Italian Renaissance. It had an exterior of pink Milford granite, Indiana limestone and terra cotta. Designed by Cady, Berg & See of New York, a firm led by the noted architect J. Cleveland Cady,[65] the new structure was greatly admired in the pages of the *Hartford Courant*:

> *It is a modern building, with all the new and approved ideas that have become a necessity of the up-to-date, light, convenient and comfortable office. The building has a handsome front of six stories, with ample windows, and the main entrance is one of the best in the city, simple in its taste and rich in white marble, mahogany woodwork, glass and brass trimmings.*

The company initially occupied the entire second floor of the building, renting out the remaining space to other prominent financial institutions.[66] The building was enlarged in 1910 with an addition in the rear and more space reserved for the company's own use, but business grew so rapidly that the company began to use offices in various parts of the building that were intended to be leased or had recently been vacated. This resulted in the company's offices being scattered throughout the building, with various sections of a single department "found in widely separated parts of different floors." To remedy the situation, the company decided to consolidate offices on four floors in 1915.[67] Five years

Phoenix Mutual Life Insurance Company Building, Pearl Street. *Hartford Collection, Hartford History Center, Hartford Public Library.*

later, the company moved to its newly built building on Elm Street. In 1924, the old property was sold to Foster E. Harvey, of Harvey & Lewis opticians, who added a new upper story to the building.[68] Today, Phoenix Mutual Life Insurance occupies its famous two-sided building at One American Row and a parking garage stands on the site of the old Pearl Street home.

THE JUDD BUILDING AND THE DIME SAVINGS BANK

Two other buildings destroyed for the same parking garage were the Judd Building and the Dime Savings Bank, both built in the early 1920s. They replaced an earlier four-story building that occupied the block of Pearl between the Phoenix Mutual Life Building on the east and Lewis Street and the National Fire Insurance Building on the west. The Judd Building, a nine-story office tower, was built in 1923–24 at Seventy-one to Seventy-nine Pearl Street, and the Dime Savings Bank, a one-story brick Colonial structure, was built in 1925 at Sixty-five Pearl Street. Both buildings were designed by William F. Brooks, a Hartford-based architect from New Britain, and constructed by Marc Eidlitz & Son of New York.[69]

South side of Pearl Street, looking east, 1940s. *From right to left*: National Fire Insurance Company Building, Judd Building, Dime Savings Bank, Phoenix Mutual Life Building and the State Savings Bank.

The Judd Building was constructed by Judd & Company, an investment banking firm founded in 1919 by a group of partners that included a married couple, Harold L. Judd and Florence Gates Judd, née Hopwood. Born into a wealthy Minneapolis family in 1887, Florence Hopwood's first husband was Charles Gates, whose father John was famous for the invention of barbed wire. After the death of her first husband, she married Harold Judd of New Britain in 1915. Their unhappy marriage ended in divorce in 1934, and Florence Gates Judd, who owned a seat on the New York Stock Exchange, went on to establish a new company and kept an office in the Gates Building in New Britain, which she also owned. This successful single businesswoman died in 1970.[70] The Judd Building survived for a half century, until the morning of Sunday, July 29, 1973, when the building was demolished by carefully placed explosives that leveled it in ten seconds.[71]

PHOENIX FIRE INSURANCE COMPANY AND CONNECTICUT GENERAL LIFE INSURANCE COMPANY

On the other side of Pearl Street from the buildings just mentioned was an earlier structure, designed by one of America's most famous architects. The Phoenix Fire Insurance Company Building was a three-story, polychromatic brick structure, erected in 1873 at Sixty-four Pearl Street, just west of the Pearl Street Congregational Church. It was designed by Henry Hobson Richardson, who a few years later supplied the plans for the Cheney Building on Main Street, which continues today as one of Hartford's great architectural landmarks. In 1905, Phoenix Fire sold its Pearl Street building to the Connecticut General Life Insurance Company, which proceeded to erect an additional three-story section, designed by Davis & Brooks, on the west side of its new acquisition. In 1907, two tenants moved into this new section's first floor: the Dime Savings Bank and the Riverside Trust Company. The new structure was raised an additional two stories in 1920, to plans by James Gamble Rogers. Connecticut General sold the entire building in 1925, and it had several different owners and tenants over the years. It was eventually reacquired by Connecticut General, which in 1949, moved several of its departments back in order to relieve overcrowding at its home office on Elm Street. By that time the façade of the building's 1873 section had been so altered as to leave no trace of Richardson's original

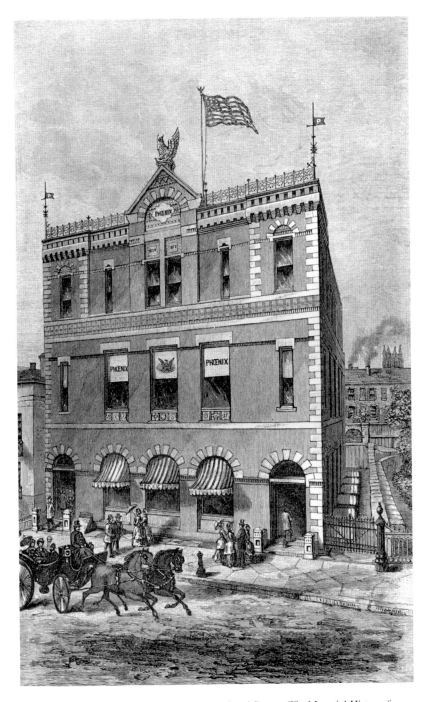

Phoenix Fire Insurance Company Building, Pearl Street. *The Memorial History of Hartford County.*

decoration. In 1950, the building was acquired by its neighbor to the west, the Mechanics Savings Bank.[72]

MECHANICS SAVINGS BANK AND ITS NEIGHBORS

The Mechanics Savings Bank was established in 1861. In 1924–25, it constructed a building at Eighty Pearl Street, previously the site of a four-story retail and tenement structure known as the Kenmore Building. The impressive Neoclassical façade of the bank's new home, designed by Morris & O'Connor of New York, featured two massive Doric columns. An expansion of the building was completed in 1953, doubling the size of the bank's lobby. Having acquired the neighboring Connecticut General property in 1950, Mechanics undertook an even more substantial expansion in 1972–73. Its original 1925 façade was retained, but the former Connecticut General Building was replaced with a very modern structure featuring decorative perforated metal panels over glass surrounded by stone aggregate. The new design was by Bernard Vinick Associates of Hartford.[73]

The remainder of the block west from the Mechanics Savings Bank to Trumbull Street was once lined with several other notable buildings. At Ninety Pearl Street stood the Renaissance façade of the 1919 Mutual Bank & Trust Company Building, designed by Isaac A. Allen Jr. Next door, at Ninety-four Pearl Street, was the façade of another classical building, designed by Smith & Bassette and built in 1925 for a brokerage firm. The Riverside Trust Company acquired the former building in 1925 and the latter one in 1937. The combined property was owned by several banks over the years and lost its earlier decorative features.[74]

By the early 1930s, Pearl Street had been thoroughly transformed from its appearance in the mid-nineteenth century. Two buildings from that era, however, had survived on the northeast corner of Pearl and Trumbull Streets, one a former residence, the other a city building. At 102 Pearl Street was an Italianate-style residence built around 1854, the former house of John B. Corning (1811–96). Corning was a Hartford merchant whose son, John J. Corning, gave the Corning Fountain in Bushnell Park to the city in memory of his father. The house was used for offices from 1913 until it was torn down in 1934 to make way for the Corning Building, a sophisticated art moderne structure designed by Lester B. Scheide. A circular medallion

Corner of Pearl and Trumbull Streets, circa 1914: Halls of Record (*left*) and Corning House (*right*). *Taylor Collection, State Archives, Connecticut State Library.*

Corner of Pearl and Trumbull Streets, circa 1984. The Halls of Record are gone and the Corning House has been replaced by the 1935 Corning Building (itself later demolished). *Library of Congress, Prints & Photographs Division.*

placed above the front entrance gave the date 1935 and bore the inscription: "Erected by the John J. Corning Estate."[75]

West of the Corning Building, on the corner of Trumbull Street, was an area that had once served as the vegetable garden for the Corning House.[76] In 1853, it became the site of an attractive two-and-a-half-story building with a mansard roof. Chiseled on the front of the building was its official title, "Halls of Record." An earlier building on Pearl Street, built in 1836, had served as the town clerk and probate offices before the Halls of Record Building was constructed.[77] As described around the turn of the century:

> *Copies of all wills and deeds of land in the City of Hartford are kept in the Halls of Record at the corner of Pearl and Trumbull street, where voters must be registered and prove themselves able to read. The offices of the Town and City Clerk, City Collector, Registrars of Voters, Judge of Probate, Board of Relief, Board of Selectmen and Board of Assessors are in this building.*[78]

These city officials moved to the new Municipal Building in 1915. During World War I, the Halls of Record served eighteen months as a draft board headquarters and then as a Soldiers, Sailors and Marines Club until it was sold by the city at auction in 1921. It was used as commercial offices until it was razed in 1940 for a parking lot.[79]

By 1989, the Mechanics Savings Bank and its neighbors to the west had all disappeared, replaced by the massive modern office complex called One Hundred Pearl Street. The new building, however, retains some surviving elements of its vanished predecessors. The columned, Classical front façade of the old Mechanics Savings Bank was incorporated into the new structure, and the medallion from the vanished Corning Building can still be seen, as it was placed on the wall of the new building near where its first home originally stood.

HARTFORD FIRE INSURANCE COMPANY

The Hartford Fire Insurance Company, commonly known today as "the Hartford," was chartered in 1810. In 1869–70, the company constructed a four-story building with a mansard roof at the northwest corner of Trumbull and Pearl Streets. Like its contemporaries, the post office and the

Hartford Fire Insurance Company Building, corner of Trumbull and Pearl Streets. *The Memorial History of Hartford County.*

Connecticut Mutual Life Building, its design was influenced by the styles of the Renaissance and French Second Empire. According to a description in the *Courant*:

> *The plan of both side and front elevations conveys the idea of great massiveness combined with remarkable elegance of outline and beauty of finish. The blocks will be deep-grooved in the seams, which will add to the appearance of solidity, and the large mouldings, wrought to a high finish.*[80]

The building was much enlarged in 1896–97, with the addition of another floor and a substantial extension on the north side. In 1899–1900, the company also constructed a five-story building on Pearl Street, adjacent to its headquarters on the west, with rental space for shops on the first floor and areas for light manufacturing above.[81] In 1931, the company moved to its current headquarters on Asylum Hill. The old building at Pearl and Trumbull Streets was demolished soon thereafter.

When searching for information about old buildings, it is not uncommon to come across accounts of unfortunate and sometimes fatal accidents. These can include fires, falls down elevator shafts and construction mishaps. On April 12, 1897, Michael J. O'Gorman, a twenty-four-year-old painter working on the west wall of the Hartford Fire Building, was killed when he fell seventy-five feet from a swinging staging. Several years earlier, Edmund C. Carter, a seventy-two-year-old worker returning from dinner to a basement vault, where he was to arrange some documents, was badly burned in a gas explosion. A pilot light on a chain gas burner had gone out, allowing the room to fill with gas. As described in the *Courant*, when Carter entered, the room was dark, so he lit a match to light the gas burner:

> *Mr. Carter was surrounded by a sheet of flame and he ran into the supply room of Barnard's printing office adjoining and fell to the floor. The employees there had hardly recovered from the shock of the explosion when they saw Mr. Carter run into the room with his clothes afire. They rushed to his assistance and extinguished the fire on his clothing, but not before it had been nearly burned from his body.*

A doctor was sent for who determined that the burns, though serious, would not prove fatal.[82]

CASE, LOCKWOOD & BRAINARD

The southwest corner of Pearl and Trumbull across from the Hartford Fire Building has had a notable history. In colonial times, it was the site of the Hartford County Jail, built in 1753, and the neighboring colony workhouse, established in 1729, where the destitute and insane could be committed. In 1793, work commenced on a new jail on the same site. It was nearing completion when, "on April 6, 1794, it was set on fire by Betsy Goodhue, an insane woman confined in one of its apartments, who perished in the flames." The brick walls were not greatly damaged in this fire, and the building was completed that autumn. The prison was on the lower level while above was a tavern called "City Hall," intended for use by the "respectable" citizens often confined in the jail for debt. In 1837, a new jail was set up farther down Pearl Street, and in 1874, the jail was removed to a new building on Seyms Street.[83]

The old 1794 jail at Pearl and Trumbull was leased (in 1838) and eventually sold (in 1841) to Case, Tiffany & Burnham, a printing firm. The business prospered in the mid-nineteenth century by producing a range of materials, including the printing and binding of many books for publishers such as Webster's Unabridged Dictionary for its first fifteen years of publication. The company was also part of Hartford's prosperous subscription publishing industry of the time, in which books were sold by agents who went door-to-door. An account of the company's history relates that

> *Mr. Burnham died in 1850…In 1853, James Lockwood and Albert G. Cooley were taken into the partnership. In 1857, Messrs. Tiffany and Cooley retired. In January, 1858, Mr. Leverett Brainard became a partner in the firm. The association of Messrs. Case, Lockwood & Brainard remained unbroken until the death of Mr. Lockwood, Jan. 13, 1888.*[84]

Business increased to such an extent during the Civil War that the company wanted to expand further. This coincided with a decision by the city to straighten Pearl Street, a project that required the tearing down of the old jail. Case, Lockwood & Brainard planned to replace the jail with a new five-story building. In 1865, the company's first step was to erect a structure just south of the jail called the City Bindery. The next year, work began on the building that would replace the jail itself. On Tuesday, May 2, 1866, workers excavating its cellar dug very close to the bindery, right up to its north wall. There was a heavy rain that night and at about 2:00 a.m. on

Corner of Pearl and Trumbull Streets, circa 1865. The Old Jail is in the center. To its left is the City Bindery. On the right is the 1836 carriage repository. The Colonial History of Hartford, *by William DeLoss Love.*

Case, Lockwood & Brainard Company Building, corner of Pearl and Trumbull Streets. This is the same corner depicted in the last image. *The Memorial History of Hartford County.*

Wednesday, the north wall fell with a loud crash that woke nearby residents, who assumed an earthquake had struck. Everyone was grateful the incident had occurred at an hour when the building was not filled with employees. The damage was significant, but the south wall was still standing. Workers who arrived the next day by way of the park did not realize at first that anything unusual had happened until they entered the building. Construction soon resumed, and the company occupied its completed home until 1927. When Hartford's publishing business declined after the Civil War, the company continued as a printer for local industries and organizations. It also produced such products as blank books and calendar pads for the general public. Beautifully designed with a rounded corner facing the intersection of Pearl and Trumbull, the Case, Lockwood & Brainard Building was demolished in 1928 for a temporary parking lot.[85]

WEST TO THE YMCA

The western stretch of Pearl Street to its end, across from Bushnell Park, was somewhat slower to develop than the built-up section between Main and Trumbull. Among the notable lost structures in this section was the 1886 factory of the Plimpton Manufacturing Company, which produced envelopes and stationery. In 1922, the factory was replaced by a new building (252 Pearl Street) that housed the company's store and printing department until 1947. On the south side of Pearl Street, the Southern New England Telephone Company (SNET) had two buildings. A three-story Renaissance-revival building, built around 1890 at 251 Pearl Street, survives today, but a six-story building, built by the company in 1911 at 185 Pearl Street, does not. The latter structure was built just west of the Case, Lockwood & Brainard Building, on the site of an 1836 carriage repository, which was later used as a chair factory. A seven-story addition was made to the 1911 building in 1920, but the need for more space did not abate, and SNET built again a decade later, this time a six-story building at 55 Trumbull Street, which was raised an additional six stories in 1953. Unlike its predecessor, this building survives today and has been converted into apartments.[86]

At the end of Pearl Street, on the corner of Ford Street across from Bushnell Park, once stood one of Hartford's greatest architectural landmarks. Built in 1893, architect Edward T. Hapgood's Romanesque design for the YMCA Building made it resemble a turreted fortress. It was well situated on a corner in a picturesque juxtaposition with the Soldiers and Sailors Memorial Arch, Bushnell Park and the Park River. In 1914, it expanded, with an addition that complemented the original architecture. Containing a pool and gymnasiums, the addition was built at an angle from the main building to correspond with the southeast curve of the property along Jewel Street.

This new section was replaced in 1938 with a Colonial revival structure that survives today. Even at that time there was a desire to replace the old 1893 building. By the late 1960s, the YMCA considered it obsolete and hazardous. It was partly condemned in 1970. Three years later, with its demolition imminent, a newly formed citizens group called the Hartford Architecture Conservancy sought to save the historic structure. The building's destruction was delayed in early 1974 while the YMCA studied the matter, but razing the old building was considered necessary for future expansion. That March, the Architecture Conservancy maintained a daily vigil in front of the endangered structure, but in spite of a delay while the YMCA satisfied the city's insistence on additional public liability insurance, the building finally met its end.[87] Since then, the spot has remained a parking lot.

CHAPTER FOUR

ASYLUM STREET'S LOST ARCHITECTURAL TREASURES

A block north of Pearl Street is another important business route. Asylum Street, which parallels the westward path of Pearl, has been the site of some of Hartford's most prominent lost landmarks. Traversing the street today, travelers find a number of tall modern buildings and many parking lots that were once home to rows of vanished buildings. In spite of the losses, Asylum Street does have a number of surviving early buildings that give a sense of how the entire street would have appeared a century and more ago.

The block between Main and Trumbull Streets has been particularly hard hit. Today, it has a long parking lot for most of its north side. At the corner of Trumbull Street, however, is a brownstone building (190 Trumbull Street), built in 1860 by the Charter Oak Bank. The south side has the 1929 Corning Building (811 Main Street) at the corner of Main Street and a series of smaller buildings, some dating to the nineteenth century, near the intersection with Trumbull Street. One of these is Cone's Building (89 Asylum Street), built in 1873 by the J.H. & W.E. Cone Hardware Company and much altered since then. At the corner with Trumbull Street is a building dating to about 1855, constructed by Timothy M. Allyn, proprietor of the Allyn House Hotel. In the late nineteenth and early twentieth centuries, this stretch was lined with many similar commercial blocks, making it an active retail area supporting a number of businesses, including several prominent clothiers.

The old Catlin Building, corner of Main and Asylum Streets, circa 1896. *Taylor Collection, State Archives, Connecticut State Library.*

CATLIN'S CORNER AND THE HARTFORD NATIONAL BANK

The northwest corner of Main and Asylum Streets, once called Catlin's Corner, witnessed some interesting transformations over the years. For many years it was the site of an old commercial structure called the Catlin Building. It was built in the early nineteenth century by Henry L. Ellsworth and was later owned by Julius Catlin.[88] The trustees of the Julius Catlin Estate planned to replace it with a new building in 1897. Before the work could begin, however, they were confronted by the city street board's desire to increase the width of Asylum Street at that corner. As one official put it, "The opportunity to relieve this congested point before the proposed new building should be erected should not be allowed to pass without the city taking advantage of it."[89] The trustees agreed to alter their plans for the building, which was designed by William C. Brocklesby. Instead of having an acute angle, the southeast corner would curve, providing additional sidewalk space.[90]

In addition to street traffic, this busy area had become the favored place where pedestrians gathered to board trolley cars heading west. One contemporary, whose views on "The Asylum Street Corner" appeared in the *Hartford Courant* on April 9, 1897, noted that the "crowding of people

Catlin Building, corner of Main and Asylum Streets, circa 1899. *Hartford Collection, Hartford History Center, Hartford Public Library.*

at the corner of Asylum street is less endurable than hitherto, now that the Catlin Building is being taken down." This observer lamented the fact that "the Asylum street habit has become chronic here in Hartford," even though there was ample waiting space available on nearby street corners. "There is plenty of room, if only the people would occupy it." One solution to the problem suggested itself:

> *Several who have thought of the matter favor some sort of public accommodation, at public expense, on City Hall Square. The latest and simplest suggestion is to widen the sidewalk on the northwest side of the square and cover a strip of it to keep off the sun and rain. This is the best way yet evident, if the city is going to assume responsibility for the crowd and feels itself bound to look out for people who are waiting for a car to come along.*

A variation of this last notion was eventually brought to fruition. In 1909, Alderman Thomas Russell made the initial proposal that the city set up a roped-off enclosure on State Street, north of the Old State House (then used as city hall), where trolley passengers could wait in safety from traffic. It was not until 1912 that the city finally acted on the idea, setting up an "Isle of Safety." The following year, the city raised the Isle of Safety above the level of the street and then added a Mediterranean-style roofed shelter with terra cotta tiles, completed in early 1914. The Isle of Safety remained a Hartford landmark until it was removed in 1976. The structure was saved and eventually found a new home at the Connecticut Trolley Museum in East Windsor.[91]

In 1899, the new Catlin Building, completed two years earlier, revealed that there were dangers other than the traffic. As reported in the *Courant* on June 8 ("Stone Fell Out"), a fatal accident was narrowly avoided when one of the coping stones over a second-floor window fell out of place and

dropped about twenty-five feet to the sidewalk, striking near a little girl that was passing, but injuring no one. The stone was about two feet long and eight inches in thickness, and was a heavy piece of rock to be dropping about indiscriminately upon sidewalks.

George O. Sawyer's dry goods store occupied the building until 1900, at which point its interior was remodeled by Brocklesby, with stores on the first floor and offices above.[92] In 1907, it was purchased by the Hartford National Bank. This was Hartford's oldest bank, having been founded in 1792. Its longtime home was a building on State Street, built in 1811, across from the Old State House.[93]

In 1911, the bank decided to construct a new building at Catlin's corner. On June 9, 1911, a headline in the *Courant* read: "Catlin Building Is Coming Down." In existence for little over a decade, it was to be made "flat as a pancake" within a month:

Work has been in process in the Catlin building since the beginning of the week, but the fact did not become widely noticed until yesterday, when the bridge over the sidewalk on Asylum street was put up and glass in the windows on the first floor was removed.

The new building, designed by Donn Barber, is considered to have been Hartford's first skyscraper. It consisted of a large banking floor (taking up the equivalent of two stories) with nine stories above for offices. It was a steel-framed structure, with a granite basement, limestone on the lower section and the rest displaying tapestry brick. The banking area consisted of two mezzanines, the second used only for ventilation, making it effectively "an air storehouse." Like the Catlin Building before it, the new skyscraper had a gracefully rounded corner facing the intersection of Main and Asylum. A *Courant* story entitled "Hartford National Bank in Its Handsome New Home," which appeared on September 20, 1912, described it:

> *The Hartford National Bank, the oldest banking institution in this section of the country, and the Main and Asylum street corner, the best known street corner in Connecticut's Capitol [sic] City, linked their fortunes together yesterday, and henceforth it is likely that the "Hartford National Bank corner" will be the prevailing designation of that busy spot in this city's life…As Asylum street is the first street with which the stranger becomes familiar, so the new bank building is the first structure, unless it be the State Capitol, to attract the stranger's eye. The flatiron building in New York possesses a similar focal vantage point in that city's business center as does this structure to the business life of Hartford.*

The Hartford National Bank became the Hartford-Aetna National Bank in 1915. It vacated its 1912 building in 1927 after another merger made it the Hartford National Bank and Trust. The building was then rented out by the Hartford-Aetna Realty Corporation, and the former banking space was divided into two stores.[94] By 1989, the building was owned by Society for Savings, which planned to erect a massive new office tower on the site. In spite of the efforts of preservationists, the building was demolished on June 2, 1990. The proposed building was never constructed, and the area remains a parking lot to this day.

ALLYN HOUSE AND ALLYN HALL

For over a century, the northwest corner of Asylum and Trumbull, where Hartford 21 and part of the XL Center stand today, was the site of the Allyn House, a fashionable hotel built by the Hartford businessman and entrepreneur Timothy M. Allyn (1800–1882), who served as mayor of Hartford from 1858 to 1860. In 1853, plans for the building were drawn by Hartford architect Octavius J. Jordan.[95] It was to have a quadrangle, with a courtyard in the center and brownstone exterior walls facing Trumbull and Asylum Streets, "both elevations having a massive and imposing appearance." On the roof, visitors would be able to admire the view from a balustrade walk. The main floor would have parlors and drawing rooms. The *Courant* described the structure:

> *In front of the office, in the main halls, will be handsome Corinthian columns, surmounted with arches springing from column to column. There will be eleven fine stores under the main floor of the Hotel, and basement stores underneath. The Building will be four stories high on two wings and five stories high on the west wing. The north wing will be devoted to the culinary department, the arrangements for which are very complete. In the second, third and fourth stories are fine suites of rooms for families.*[96]

Construction began in 1856 and was completed the following year, when the hotel could finally be described firsthand:

> *The public entrance is on Asylum street, with a private entrance for ladies on Trumbull Street. The most striking feature, on entering the halls of the hotel, is the broad stair case, with a flight of stairs for the gentlemen on the one side, and the ladies on the other, meeting at the various landings, and parting as each story is approached. There will be some chance meetings on those landings, that will send shocks of something as stirring as electricity, through the human frame. The consequences will go down to posterity. The ladies and gents meet to part a few times—but finally meet to part no more.*

The dining room ran the whole length of the west side and had a flight of stairs for ladies to slip out quietly, unless they chose to "take the grand parade past the office, and the gentlemen-loungers in the corridors." The *Courant* congratulated Mr. Allyn, stating "that our whole community owes him hearty thanks for his public spirited effort to supply what we have long needed, a hotel in every respect of the first class."[97]

After Timothy M. Allyn died in 1882, the hotel was expanded by his successors, who built an annex to the north on Trumbull Street. This addition blocked from view and partly incorporated the Allyn family residence where Abraham Lincoln had stayed with Mayor Allyn in 1860.[98] This early nineteenth-century house had previously been the residence of one Edward Goodwin. As a longtime resident of Hartford recalled in 1899, the old mansion

> *stood on the corner of Trumbull, quite a distance back from both streets, a sightly place surrounded by trees and shrubbery, including*

The Allyn House Hotel, corner of Trumbull and Asylum Streets. Allyn Hall (later the Auditorium Building) is on the left. *Library of Congress, Prints & Photographs Division, Detroit Publishing Company Collection.*

several catalpa trees, bearing long slender pods similar to vanilla leaves, which the boys used to gather, and after drying, smoked in imitation of cigars.[99]

The Allyn House hotel was extensively remodeled in 1898–99 to plans by Isaac A. Allen Jr. The entrances on Trumbull and Asylum were altered to be at street level and led into a new and lavishly ornate lobby, enlarged by the removal of some of the ground-floor retail space. The back of the lobby was the former open courtyard, now under a gilded domed ceiling with a large skylight. The hotel also now had a separate ladies' restaurant and a gentlemen's café. Rooms were also set up where traveling salesmen could display samples. Accessible from the lobby, these rooms were in what had previously been the old Allyn residence.[100]

The building's time as a luxury hotel ended in 1920, when much of it was converted to commercial use. It still managed to attract a notable guest, even with its reduced rates, when the famously parsimonious Calvin Coolidge, then vice president, spent a night in the hotel. The Allyn House was finally torn down in 1960, and the space was used as a parking lot until the Civic Center (now the XL Center) was built in the 1970s.[101]

Timothy M. Allyn's efforts to supply the city with needed buildings did not end with the Allyn House. In 1860, he built Allyn's Hall, just west of the Allyn House and connected to it by a bridge on the second floor. Designed by Octavius J. Jordan, it had a large public hall (four times as large as Union Hall), as well as shops. It also contained the armory of the First Company, Governor's Foot Guard, which moved to its present armory in 1888. Allyn's Hall was the scene of many political debates and party conventions over the years. Until Robert's Opera House opened in 1869, Allyn Hall was also Hartford's leading playhouse and a stage for lectures and readings by such luminaries as Charles Dickens, Mark Twain, Horace Greeley and Henry Ward Beecher. In later years, it was used for dances, sporting events, vaudeville theater and, finally, as a movie house. It became known as the Auditorium Building after its purchase by Patrick Donaghue in 1894. One of the Donaghue Brothers, who were wholesale liquor dealers, he invested in much prime downtown real estate at the time. In 1905, Donaghue sold the auditorium to W.W. Walker, a grocer, who had plans to eventually remodel the building for that business.[102] This change never took place. On February 26, 1914, the building was destroyed in a massive fire. As the *Courant* reported the following day ("Big Crowd Sees Structure Burn"), a huge crowd gathered to watch the unfolding events, filling up nearby streets (some even went onto the roofs of neighboring buildings). A large number of policemen were needed to hold them back. The story described the scene:

Hundreds surged against the ropes in excitement when the firemen were seen performing their dangerous tasks. A horrified gasp went up from the crowd when the front of the building was seen to collapse with a group of firemen apparently beneath it, and in the moment of suspense that followed, they held their breath in anxiety. Except for the crackling of the flames, the shouts of the firemen and the roaring of the engines under a full head of steam, hardly a sound could be heard from the spectators. When, however, it was learned that all had escaped, a sound of relief went up from the crowd. One woman fainted and was carried into a store nearby.

South side of Asylum Street. The building labeled "Sanders House" was the birthplace of J.P. Morgan. *Taylor Collection, State Archives, Connecticut State Library.*

Part of the old wall of the destroyed auditorium was reused for the Majestic Theater, which was built on the same site in 1915. Designed by Isaac J. Allen Jr., it was an up-to-date structure and immediately attracted attention with its brilliantly lit electric sign. This building was demolished in the early 1960s, not long after its neighbor, the Allyn House.[103]

WHERE J.P. MORGAN WAS BORN

When the Allyn House was built, it was considered to be "out in the country," but Asylum Street west of Trumbull Street developed rapidly in the second half of the nineteenth century. As the *Courant* noted in 1860:

> *It will not be many years before Asylum street will be occupied entirely by the marts of trade. Business began to work west of Trumbull street with something like hesitation. Silas Andrus & Son built their block near High street, contrary to the advice of business men who knew "a thing or two." It proved to have been a wise movement, and others are following those who succeeded the Messrs. Andrus in this direction.*[104]

69

This part of Asylum was still residential when the famous banker, financier and philanthropist J. Pierpont Morgan was born there on April 17, 1837, in the house of his grandfather, Joseph Morgan. The house was altered to serve as a block of stores around 1860. The adjacent house, home of Dr. George Sumner, on the corner of Trumbull Street had already been replaced by a brownstone business block, built in 1856 by the dry goods firm of Day, Owen & Company. Other buildings were soon built to the west, on the estate of Major James Goodwin (1803–1878), who was one of Hartford's leading businessmen at that time. This land was developed in the early 1880s by his sons, James J. Goodwin and Reverend Francis Goodwin, who were cousins of J.P. Morgan. In 1881, they laid out Haynes Street through the property and, on its corner with Asylum, constructed the Goodwin Building, which had stores on the first floor and luxury apartments above. It was here that J.P. Morgan would stay on his return visits to Hartford. Designed by Francis Kimball and Thomas Wisedell of New York, the ornate terra cotta façade of the Goodwin Building survives today, incorporated into the Goodwin Square office tower, which was completed in 1989. On the opposite (east) side of Haynes Street from the Goodwin Building, the brothers built a new commercial building in 1890–91, designed by Hartford architect George Keller.[105]

As described above, the houses on the south side of Asylum, between Trumbull Street and the future Haynes Street, were mostly replaced by commercial building between 1856 and 1891. This block would see further changes in the 1920s. A seven-story building was constructed in 1924 at 173–183 Asylum Street for the Plaut Company, a furniture store, which went out of business in 1932. In 1933, the Garber Brothers furniture company moved in, and in 1942, yet another furniture store, the Flint-Bruce Company, bought the building. Just to the east, the house in which J.P. Morgan was born was acquired by the Garber Brothers in 1926. They and their partners demolished it and built a new six-story building called, appropriately, the Morgan Building, at 151–165 Asylum Street. Opened in 1928, its façade had a Gothic design by Hartford architects Ebbets and Frid, with marble on the first two floors and cast stone above. The lower floors were rented for stores while the four upper floors originally contained bowling alleys and later offices. In 1960, the building became the home of the Resolute Insurance Group, which renamed it the Resolute Building.[106]

Sandwiched in the narrow lot between the two 1920s buildings was a highly ornamented nineteenth-century structure at 167–169 Asylum Street. It had been home to a number of businesses over the decades, including the

Vienna Bakery and the Ailing Rubber Company. All three of these buildings were removed in the 1980s to make way for the City Place Development.

Just west of Haynes Street and the Goodwin Building, on the south side of Asylum Street, are three buildings (235–257 Asylum Street) that survive from the 1870s, built by the developer John Harrison. Others to the west were lost in the twentieth century, including the building at 265 Asylum Street, which from 1874 to 1917 was the home of the John N. Ney Company, makers of dental gold. It was removed in 1921, when Ann Street was extended south to Pearl Street, right through where the old building had stood. The next building west, constructed in 1870 for the Talcott Brothers drug and chemical firm, was replaced by the current building in 1926. Next is a surviving building, constructed in 1877–1878 by William Boardman & Sons, dealers in coffee, tea and spices, who had an even more elaborate building, now lost, directly across the street. From this building west, there is today a parking lot.[107]

THE HARTFORD LIFE INSURANCE COMPANY AND THE FIRST HARTFORD HIGH SCHOOL

At the northeast corner of Asylum and Ann Streets (Ann was renamed Ann Uccello Street in 2006 in honor of Hartford's first female mayor and the first female mayor of a state capital city) is part of the large structure of the XL Center. In the mid-nineteenth century, an old house on this site was home to Thomas Church Brownell (1779–1865), who served as the third presiding bishop of Connecticut, the seventh presiding bishop of the United States Episcopal Church and the first president of Trinity College. By the 1890s, the yard of the house had been hemmed in by one-story commercial blocks. In 1897, the Hartford Life Insurance Company, first chartered in 1866, completed a beautiful and highly ornamented building of granite, limestone, pressed brick and architectural ironwork, designed by F.R. Comstock. In 1913, the company merged with the Missouri State Life Insurance Company and moved out of Hartford. The building (252 Asylum Street) passed through other owners, and in 1944, it became the first Hartford location of the legendary Frank's Restaurant. For decades, Frank's was a gathering place for Hartford politicians and businessmen. The restaurant would have three homes in the city before it closed in 1995. It was forced to move out of the old Hartford Life Building when it was gutted in a fire in 1963 and torn down.[108]

Hartford's first high school building was constructed at the northwest corner of Asylum and Ann Streets in 1847. It was a simple three-story brick structure, with a gable roof facing Asylum Street, and had desks for about three hundred students. The move to build the school was sparked by the publication in 1846 of a tract by Hartford's famed education reformer Henry Barnard entitled, "Considerations Respecting a High School in Hartford."[109] The new High School was combined with a much older institution, Hartford's Grammar School, which went back to 1638. According to Henry Barnard, the school "was built after more than ordinary search for the best plan, (a committee having visited Boston, Lowell, Salem, Newburyport, Worcester, Providence, and Middletown, for this purpose)." It was designed for both boys and girls, and its location "is at once central, and large enough for the appropriate yards." The first and second floors had classrooms, and the upper floor was devoted to a hall:

This is appropriated to reading, and declamation, and for the female department of the school, to daily recess, and calisthenic exercises. A moderately raised platform is located at one end, above which an extended blackboard is placed, and settees are ranged around the walls; these, properly arranged, together with the settees from the lower rooms, which are easily transported above, speedily convert the open Hall into a commodious Lecture room,—and also adapt it to the purposes of public examinations and exhibitions.[110]

A new high school was built on Hopkins Street in 1869, and the property at Asylum and Ann Streets was sold the next year to Foster & Company, wholesale grocery dealers. In 1871, the company built an impressive five-story commercial block on the site, with a French mansard roof and a façade of Philadelphia pressed brick. Patrick Donaghue, the wholesale liquor dealer who was mentioned above as owning a number of valuable properties in the city, bought the Foster Block in 1905. An Irish immigrant, Donaghue renamed the building the Weldon, his wife's maiden name and his son's given name. The building had various tenants over the years. Later acquired by the Roman Catholic Archdiocese of Hartford, it was torn down in 1982 for a parking lot.[111]

THE BATTERSON BUILDING AND
THE HOTEL GARDE

West of the site of the Weldon Building is the former Bond Hotel, which was built in two sections in 1913 and 1921. Asylum Street continues west, past the intersection with High Street, passes the northern end of Bushnell Park to the south and then crosses under the train tracks, after which it becomes Asylum Avenue. Of the notable lost buildings along this stretch, perhaps the most impressive was the Batterson Building, which once dominated the northeast corner of Asylum and High Streets. It was constructed by James G. Batterson, founder of Travelers Insurance, who purchased the land in 1866. It had been the site of Thrall's screw factory, which had burned down a decade earlier, leaving an empty lot.[112] Batterson, a builder and owner of a granite quarry, constructed an ornate brick business block with a French mansard roof and a corner tower. In 1905–6, the building was altered by William H. Garde to become the Hotel Garde. It was related in the *Hartford Courant* in 1913 that

> *the name of Garde has been connected with hotels in Connecticut for many years and in a most successful and honorable manner. The late William H. Garde made of the Garde in New Haven a hotel known far and wide for its accommodations and its spirit of hospitality, and Mr. Garde was favorably known to a large clientele. It was for him that the Hotel Garde in Hartford was built* [renovated], *but an accident during the work of fitting the building to its new purpose led to his death before the new undertaking was well under way.*

William Henry Garde suffered a severe fall on December 2, 1905, from which he never recovered, dying a little over a year later. The management of the hotel passed to his widow and his son, Walter S. Garde. In 1913, management of the hotel was taken over by Ernest H.G. Meyer. His son, Fred H. Meyer, took over in 1916, but by 1918, the hotel was bankrupt.[113] It was soon acquired by a group of new owners, led by Thomas G. Hardie, who planned to divide most of the spacious lobby into stores. Many long-standing patrons of the hotel objected, and the decision was changed: "It was found that the comfortable lounge room facing directly on a busy street had been, and is, a great drawing card for traveling salesmen who have made the hotel their stopping place for many years."[114]

The hotel passed through many other managers over the years and was remodeled several times. It survived a three-alarm fire in 1943, but the construction of the nearby Hotel Statler in 1954 (which has also since been demolished) cut into business. In January 1970, the heating system failed, forcing out the dilapidated building's ninety-eight residents, most of whom were seniors living on welfare allowances. In spite of attempts to save it by the newly formed Hartford Architecture Conservancy, the venerable hotel was demolished in 1973.[115] A modern red brick building now occupies the site: Capitol Center, built in 1981.

CHAPTER FIVE

GROWTH AND DEVELOPMENT OF THREE HARTFORD DEPARTMENT STORES

M ain Street, from Asylum Street north to Talcott Street, was long home to a number of important department stores. These businesses have long since vanished, but some of the buildings they occupied still exist today. A few of the most famous are the former G. Fox & Company Building at 960 Main Street, the Sage-Allen Building at 884 Main Street (later significantly altered to become a retail and apartment block, called the Lofts at Main and Temple) and between them, the Richardson Building, formerly called the Cheney Building, that at one time was home to Brown, Thomson & Company. On the other side of Main Street is One American Plaza, at 915 Main Street, former home of Wise, Smith & Company. Other buildings, such as the Hartford branch of Steiger's—a Springfield-based department store—have been demolished. This chapter looks at the histories of the G. Fox, Sage-Allen and Wise, Smith & Company Buildings to show the contrasting ways in which these stores grew from humble beginnings to expansive showplaces. In doing so, they supplanted a number of interesting lost buildings.

TWO FIRES AND G. FOX & COMPANY

In business from 1847 to 1993, G. Fox & Company grew to become Hartford's premiere department store and the largest privately owned department store in the country. The store was founded by Gerson Fox (1811–1880), a Jewish immigrant from Germany, who started a fancy goods store that sold notions such as ribbon, thread, lace and gloves. The store then grew as a dry goods business and later into a department store under the leadership of Gerson's son, Moses Fox (1850–1938), and his granddaughter, Beatrice Fox Auerbach (1887–1968).[116] In 1965, Auerbach sold the store to a national chain. It finally closed in 1993. In the course of the company's growth, two fires, one in 1887 and the other in 1917, would have a great impact.

Having occupied various rented locations on Main Street for thirty-three years, G. Fox & Company erected a new building of its own in 1880–81. Designed by J. Bachmeyer, it stood at 406–410 Main Street, just north of the Cheney Building. Its front was built of Philadelphia pressed brick with Ohio stone trimmings and was surmounted by an elaborate metallic cornice.[117] Gerson Fox did not live to see the four-story building completed.

North of the Fox Building was a structure known as the Averill Building. It consisted of two connected houses that were built in 1824 and later converted to stores with tenements above. On January 9, 1887, this building was destroyed in a fire that originated in the coal furnace and quickly spread. It was one of the coldest nights of the winter, and it took seven minutes to get water, which had frozen, from the Temple Street hydrant. According to one account:

There were those near before water could be got on [who] *saw ugly puffs of smoke curling out* [of] *the gratings under the showcases in the front of the building, and a moment later the smoke curled up on the inside of the building, wreathed against the plate glass window, there was a loud crash as of an explosion, and the whole glass front of the store flew out upon the sidewalk.*[118]

A crowd of thousands of onlookers, undeterred by the freezing temperatures, watched the dramatic events from the street below. The *Hartford Times* reported:

When the flames were running up the cornice on the outside of the building Mrs. Forbes and Miss Shea appeared at the window directly over the store. A fireman went up, took Mrs. Forbes down the ladder and told Miss Shea he would come again for her. But she gathered her skirts and followed the fireman and Mrs. Forbes down the ladder alone. She preferred to have no further delay, as matters were decidedly serious.

Thomas R. Laughton, a clerk of the fire board and city reporter for the *Hartford Times*, died from smoke inhalation after he entered the burning building. He was found by firemen and taken next door to the Cheney Building but could not be revived. Assistant engineer Louis Krug told the *Times*:

> *Tom made a great miscalculation in his attempt to ascertain the origin of the fire. As ready as he always was to face danger, I never thought he would have taken such chances. I would rather have seen the whole building burned to a cinder than see so terrible a blow to Tom and his family.* [119]

The neighboring G. Fox Building suffered damage, mostly from water. A new Averill Building was soon built on the site to replace the "unsightly" ruins, whose "tottering walls and charred timbers" had "become an eyesore." Designed by T.G. Glover of Brooklyn, it was three stories high and had a façade of Philadelphia pressed brick with terra cotta and brownstone trimmings. The first floor contained three stores, and above was a space reserved as the Odd Fellows' Hall. [120] Moses Fox acquired the building for his expanding store in 1891. The Odd Fellows retained their hall until 1902, when Fox needed the additional space. By that time, the company had also acquired the next building to the north, formerly occupied by Neal, Goff & Inglis (which had also suffered a fire in 1894). G. Fox & Company now had a lengthy frontage along Main Street.

G. Fox continued in its expanded quarters until January 29, 1917, when a fire destroyed its group of buildings, as well as the adjacent Woolworth's store. The fire also threatened the neighboring Cheney Building, home of the Brown Thomson department store, which survived. The fire started on the first floor around 11:00 p.m. and soon engulfed the structure. Every available engine and pumper in the city arrived, and firemen fought the blaze at close range, endangered by falling windows and timbers and with the fear that the west wall might fall into Main Street.

The fire started shortly after the theaters let out, "and for a time policemen found great difficulty in controlling the ever-growing crowd of men and women, many of the latter in opera cloaks, straining at the ropes to secure a point of vantage to see the blaze." At one point, the surging crowd broke down the guard rope and police had to push them back to the safety mark. Many well-dressed men jumped in to aid the firemen in setting their hoses. On the Talcott Street side of the fire, sightseers who had slipped past the police cordon pitched in to tear down flaming awnings from a neighboring building and were drenched by the firefighters' hoses in the process. As with the 1887 fire, temperatures were freezing, and walking became hazardous for onlookers as the icy streets flooded with water. Sparks as large as a man's head fell onto nearby buildings. The *Hartford Courant* reported:

> *Men, women and children, alert to prevent the spreading of the fire to the tenement houses, stood armed with axes, brooms and almost everything conceivable to beat out the small fires that repeatedly started as a result of the great sparks that were flying in every direction.*[121]

The mood of the watching crowd often swung from subdued calm to loud excitement:

> *At one moment voices would be hushed until one could actually hear the beating of the water from the hose on the inside walls of the buildings. And then the whistle of one of the engines would seem to act as a safety valve for all the pent-up excitement and from the throng would come a roar that drowned out everything else.*[122]

A number of walls crashed down, but the walls on the Main Street side did not collapse. Firemen worked through the night to end the fire using powerful electric floodlights provided by the Hartford Electric Light Company. The debris continued to smolder for several days afterward, and firefighters were called several times to put out newly discovered patches of fire. A detail was then left to watch over the scene and keep the water pumping all night. An investigation determined that a careless night watchman was responsible for the blaze, which caused $750,000 of damages.[123]

The fire gave G. Fox the opportunity to build a new, impressive and fireproof eleven-story building, designed by Cass Gilbert of New York. It towered above its immediate neighbors at the time and showed that the company was now well placed to enter its golden era. In the 1930s, Beatrice Fox Auerbach would update the store's interiors in the art deco style and was the first among her competitors to add air-conditioning. She also added a long street-level art deco canopy, which has become a landmark in its own right. The building was physically enlarged over the years. In 1918, it was connected by a bridge above the street to the store's warehouse, built that same year on the opposite side of Talcott Street. G. Fox's many departments and dedication to customer service made it legendary. When it finally closed its doors in 1993, one of Hartford's greatest institutions vanished. The building still sits on the site of the earlier structures destroyed in the 1887

After the G. Fox & Company fire in 1917. On the left are the Pilgard Building, built in 1911, and the First Baptist Church, built in 1856. On the right is a corner of the Cheney Building. *Hartford Collection, Hartford History Center, Hartford Public Library.*

and 1917 fires and today continues as a downtown landmark. It now serves as the home of Capitol Community College.

SAGE, ALLEN & COMPANY, THE OLD MANSION HOUSE AND THE BALLERSTEIN BUILDING

In 1889, Jerome E. Sage, Normand F. Allen and Clifford O. Moore formed the dry goods firm of Sage, Allen & Company, which occupied space in the building at the northwest corner of Main and Trumbull Streets. For many years, the building had been the home of Talcott & Post, a firm that sold dry goods and carpets. In 1881 the two partners split up. C.M. Talcott continued to operate the dry goods business at the old location, but William H. Post opened a new store, farther north on the opposite side of Main Street (later home to Neal, Goff & Inglis), where he sold carpets, curtains and wallpaper. Talcott retired in 1889 and sold his building to Moses and Leopold Fox, who leased it to Sage, Allen & Company.[124] On April 22, 1889, the *Hartford Courant* reported on "Sage, Allen & Company's New Store," noting that *the store has been entirely refitted, and is now one of the best lighted and most attractive establishments of the kind to be found in the city. A new departure is made in the way of exterior showcases, fitted with movable arms, so arranged as to admit of a most advantageous display of the contents.*

In a story entitled "Of Interest to Every One" (July 10, 1889), the paper observed that

the success of this popular house since it was started a short time since has been wonderful. The reasons, however, are apparent. An excellent stock of new goods, reasonable prices, and the employment of polite and accommodating clerks who thoroughly understand their business and give careful attention to the wants of customers, have made the store a veritable rendezvous for ladies and others who are in search of dress goods, cloaks, trimmings or anything in the line of dry or fancy goods.

The store specialized in a higher order of goods that cost a bit more but gave the establishment a reputation for quality merchandise. Reporting on the Christmas shopping season "In Hartford's Stores," on December 16, 1890, the *Courant* declared, "One feels that he has gotten into a particularly nice establishment when he enters Sage, Allen & Company's store."

Across the street, Sage, Allen & Company's neighbor was Hart, Merriam & Company, dealers in carpets, oilcloths and wallpaper. In 1881, this company had moved into the building at 364 Main Street, opposite the head of Pratt Street. As the *Hartford Courant* noted ("Hart, Merriam & Company") on February 12, 1881:

By deciding upon the store which they will open to the public this evening they not only accomplished what is essential in the way of accommodations, but at the same time have located in the section of Main street that is becoming the center for many of the larger mercantile houses.

The company's new home was a structure known as the Woodbridge Building. It was named for Ward Woodbridge (1771–1856), a dry goods merchant, who had been one of the wealthiest men in Hartford. In 1895, the building was acquired by Sage and Allen, who proceeded to replace it with a new eight-story fireproof structure designed by Isaac A. Allen Jr. It opened on November 1, 1898. Sage, Allen & Company occupied the basement and the first floor. Charles R. Hart & Company (L.B. Merriam had retired) was on the second floor. It is the impressive façade of this building that survives today at 884 Main Street. Moore, one of the original partners, had been skeptical of the new building. He resigned as a partner, but stayed on as manager for twenty years. In 1903, Sage retired, and Allen secured his interest in the business. Sage went on to open his own dry goods store on Pratt Street. In 1915, Allen transferred his sole ownership of the store to a corporation called Sage, Allen & Company Incorporated.[125]

Allen soon needed more space if he wished to grow his business and add new departments. As with Moses Fox, he looked at properties neighboring his store. His expansion efforts would focus on the block between Main and Market Streets, north of Kinsley Street. In early 1904, fire ravaged the Corning Building, located at the northeast corner of Main and Kinsley Streets. Allen acquired the property—a complex undertaking because ownership was divided among several heirs, one of whom was in Europe. To satisfy his immediate needs, he rapidly built a three-story structure on the site, occupied in 1905. It was designed so that additional floors could be added in the future (another floor was eventually added in 1916–17). In 1910, he added a long addition behind it, which extended down Kinsley Street. The second floor of this building was occupied by the Charles R. Hart Company. On Main Street was the jewelry store of Henry Kohn, which was sandwiched between the 1898 building and the 1905 addition. This store was now surrounded on three sides by Sage, Allen & Company property.[126]

Farther down Kinsley Street, adjacent to the 1910 addition, the company had also acquired a building known as the Old Mansion House. Sage, Allen & Company used the first floor of the building as a receiving room and the upper floors as workrooms. The Old Mansion House was a notable structure. It was built in 1796 by Dr. Apollos Kinsley, for whom Kinsley Street was named. Dr. Kinsley was an inventor who devised a rotary printing press and a "horseless carriage" powered by steam. He also invented a brick-processing machine and used the bricks that he made to construct his house.[127] The house faced east. Its former front yard was blocked by the neighboring Hartford Police Department Headquarters, located on the corner of Market Street. According to an 1880s description of the house, its front was

characterized by a liberal doorway with elliptical arched head, above a basement story standing up eight feet or more from the street. Many of the windows have splayed caps of marble ten inches high, the sills being of the same material; but the strongest interest attaches to the bricks themselves, as we find that they are in

A number of buildings in Hartford have been called the Corning Building. This one, at the corner of Main and Kinsley Streets, is pictured after it was damaged in a fire in 1904 (note the broken windows and debris around the building). On the left is the building occupied by Henry Kohn & Sons, Jewelers. *Taylor Collection, State Archives, Connecticut State Library.*

some instances of ornamental forms, noticeably in a water-table course, where a moulded projection is seen, and also in two courses marking the location of floors within. Here is shown a species of enriched running guilloche ornament with rosettes. Near the ground line the bricks are of unusual dimensions, measuring four inches in height by sixteen inches in length. On one of these, in lieu of a corner-stone, is found the brief legend, "A. Kinsley, 1796."[128]

Sage, Allen & Company, which was now commonly abbreviated as Sage-Allen, tore down the old house in 1928 and built a new five-story building, designed by Dennison & Hirons of New York. Opened on September 3, 1929, it connected to the earlier additions along Kinsley Street and added forty thousand square feet. The interior was very modern—the removal of the store's old fixtures now gave shoppers an uninterrupted view of all the retail departments on each floor. The store occupied four times as much space as it had when it first opened in its Main Street building in 1898.[129]

Expansion and development would continue in the years after World War II. In 1946, Sage-Allen announced that it would occupy all of its 1898

Department stores on the east side of Main Street, circa 1930. *From left to right*: the 1918 G. Fox & Company Building; the 1876 Cheney Building, home of Brown, Thomson & Company; the 1894 Ballerstein Building; the 1898 Sage, Allen & Company Building; Henry Kohn & Sons; and the 1905 Sage-Allen addition on the corner of Kinsley Street. Down Kinsley Street, from left to right, can be seen the 1910 Sage-Allen addition, the 1929 building that replaced the Old Mansion House and the police headquarters on Market Street. *The Connecticut Historical Society, Hartford, Connecticut.*

building, no longer renting space out to tenants. The following year the store installed six escalators. These eliminated the need for customers to wait for up and down elevators. The company finally acquired the building that housed Henry Kohn & Sons, which had long occupied space in the middle of Sage-Allen's Main Street frontage. This structure was now connected inside with the rest of the Sage-Allen complex and opened in 1951 as a gallery for watches, jewelry and silverware. In 1955, the store completed its expansion to Market Street by acquiring the old police headquarters building, built in 1898 and designed by John J. Dwyer. The police headquarters was demolished to provide parking.[130]

With one exception, Sage-Allen now occupied the entire block, bounded by Main Street on the west, Temple Street on the north, Market Street to the East and Kinsley Street to the south. The exception was the Ballerstein

The Old Mansion House on Kinsley Street. *Taylor Collection, State Archives, Connecticut State Library.*

Building, located on the northeast corner of Main and Temple. An elaborately ornamented six-story Romanesque revival structure, it was built in 1893–94 for R. Ballerstein & Company, wholesale milliners (sellers of women's hats). It was designed by F.S. Newman of Springfield, and its construction was supervised by Isaac A. Allen Jr., who was at that time in charge of Newman's Hartford office. On July 15, 1893, the *Courant* described the building, then under construction:

> *The first two stories on the front are of iron and the rest pressed buff brick with blue marble and terra cotta. A large oriel bay window takes in the third and fourth story front, and finishes with a large arch in the fifth story. The bay will contain polished plate glass windows...the main cornice will be of copper. The front gable will be filled with terra cotta carving, standing out boldly over the top of the pediment...On the Temple street corner a tower will rise two stories higher than the roof. In the upper story will be a Seth Thomas illuminated clock with three dials.*[131]

Passersby watched the erection of the Ballerstein Building with growing interest, and when the store finally opened, on March 20, 1894, a large crowd was waiting to get in. The following day, a *Courant* reporter, who had experienced the "Ballerstein Crush" firsthand, related that he had been "one of the miles of humanity who stood for just half an hour wedged in like sardines in a box, without being able to move hand or foot." People felt smothered, but "half-dead victims could get neither in nor out" until the doors opened, and "then, with a rush that was a shame to a decent gathering, the crowd jammed forward and crushed women and children until they screamed in agony." Stampedes of shoppers, like the ones witnessed each November on the day after Thanksgiving, are not a recent invention.

In 1909, Ballerstein's partner, Charles H. Dillon, acquired the business, and the building became known as the Dillon Building. In 1923, it was leased to Worth, Inc., a women's clothing store. The building was torn down for a modern two-story building in 1964.[132]

In 1967, Sage-Allen announced that the Main Street façade of its store would be getting a major face-lift. The Kohn Building was finally demolished, replaced by an addition that would unify the interior of the store on all four levels (three floors and the basement). A new brick and concrete storefront was built, to unify the store along Main Street. Unfortunately, this change covered up the Victorian-era ornamentation on the lower floors of the 1898 building. The upper floors, rising above the new façade, still displayed Isaac A. Allen Jr.'s original design.[133] In 1993, Sage-Allen closed its doors after 104 years in business. Its complex remained vacant until 2005–6, when a new apartment and retail structure was built on the site—one that retained the 1898 façade. The 1960s front was removed and the deteriorated buildings on either side were demolished. New additions on the north and south were built with minimal decoration so as not to contrast with the original architecture. This example of adaptive reuse has allowed the old façade to continue to mark the head of Pratt Street, as it has for over a century.

WISE, SMITH & COMPANY

The old Fourth Congregational Church Building on Main Street, which for decades had served as a theater with shops on the first floor, was demolished in 1897 to make way for an impressive new six-story building. This was to be the home of Wise, Smith & Company, a newly established department store. Its leader was Isidore Wise. Born in Hartford in 1865 and educated in the public schools, he began in the dry goods business as a cash boy for G. Fox, when it was still a modest notions store. He became manager at another store but declined a business offer there, and in 1888, he established his own firm, I. Wise & Company. Two years later, he bought out a store located in the center of the Cheney Building. His continued success eventually warranted a move to his own building. One of his partners in this new venture was Robert Smith, a large cloak manufacturer with stores in Manhattan, Brooklyn and Newark.[134]

Wise, Smith & Company opened on November 1, 1897. At the time, opening a department store of more than one story was considered a risky venture, and the west side of Main Street was not considered the best area for retail. However, a line of people waited in the pouring rain for the chance to get inside and see the store's seven levels, all occupied by the one firm. Each visitor to the opening received a souvenir: an etched copy of a painting in the Wadsworth Atheneum, which depicted the flagship *Hartford* in action. The tradition of distributing souvenirs would continue in later years each time the store celebrated its anniversary. Business grew rapidly under the leadership of Isidore Wise. As a civic leader in Hartford, he served as councilman, alderman and police commissioner, as well as president of Congregation Beth Israel and the United Jewish Charities. On the occasion of the store's twentieth anniversary, Isidore Wise addressed the employees and explained that the company had been a success from the beginning because "honesty, courtesy, attention to the patron's needs and desires, and justice to the patrons had made the people realize that the store was attempting to do business on a firm basis."[135]

Like G. Fox and Sage-Allen, Wise, Smith & Company soon grew to occupy adjacent buildings. In 1902, the firm leased the Roberts Block, located just to the north on Main Street. Built by William W. Roberts in 1866, this was a five-floor brownstone-fronted commercial block with a mansard roof. It originally had a Masonic Hall on an upper floor. In 1868, Roberts added an opera house at the rear, which was entered through the central hall of his building on Main Street. It was a substantial theater and the largest single building yet roofed in Hartford at the time. According to the *Courant*, Roberts took great care in planning what would, for many decades, be the city's premiere performance space:

> *While he has been negotiating for the different strips of land necessary to enable him to carry out his plans, Mr. Roberts has been carefully studying upon all the requirements for a first class music hall, such as proper proportions, tasteful ornamentation, comfortable seats, and above all good ventilation and proper facilities for ingress and egress.*[136]

Roberts Opera House rose to the front rank of theaters in the country, and many stars of the era performed there, including Sarah Bernhardt.

Upon leasing the Robert's Block, Wise made openings in the wall to connect its floors with those in the Wise, Smith & Company Building. The lease did not include the theater (by then known as the Hartford Opera House), which still had an entrance through the Roberts Block. Wise also leased the Hamersley Building on Pratt Street, located behind the store, to use as a warehouse for his new grocery department. After a fire destroyed the Hamersley Building in 1905, its owner, state supreme court judge William J. Hamersley, put up a new building to replace it. This property was acquired by Wise, Smith & Company in 1917.

In 1907, both the Roberts Block and the opera house were formally purchased by the firm. The opera house continued to be leased for several years as a theater by the Jennings & Graves Company. The department store arranged to occupy part of the opera house that had been used as a café and billiard room. The theater finally closed in 1917, and the store remodeled it for retail space.[137]

Wise, Smith & Company acquired two other properties on Main Street in the first decade of the twentieth century. North of the Roberts Block and south of Christ Church was the Miller Building. The old Hinckley Building had stood on the site until 1875, when W.M. Miller tore it down and erected a new brick structure for his own store. Covering "Opening Day at Miller's," the *Courant* noted on November 16, 1875, that "the front windows are well arranged for displaying costumes and fancy articles—the latter showing finely on a revolving pyramid, which attracts the attention of every passer." Wise, Smith & Company bought this building in 1902. The Miller Building survived until it was damaged in a fire and torn down in 1930.

Another building, just south of the Wise, Smith & Company store, was the Corning Building, once home to the dry goods business of John B. Corning. It was acquired by Isidore Wise in 1910. This purchase gave Wise, Smith & Company a total frontage of 205 feet on Main Street across all of its properties— the Corning Building, 1897 store, Roberts Block and Miller Building. The result exceeded that of any other business in the city at the time.[138] The *Courant* observed on the occasion of the store's fourteenth anniversary in 1911 that

> *expansion has been the policy of the firm not only in connection with its business, but by extending its influence to build up Hartford and the outlying districts through its improved facilities for trading, a large factor of which is its complete city and suburban delivery service.*[139]

In 1912, the Corning Building was replaced with a new nine-story building designed by Isaac A. Allen Jr. The original 1897 store was raised to nine stories to match it. The completed structure had a uniform façade, incorporating the old and new buildings. The front had "columns of light gray pressed brick with caps and bases of Indiana limestone, and panels and mullions of copper." At the level of the seventh floor was displayed the name "Wise-Smith & Company."[140]

In 1917, Wise added to his properties on Pratt Street by acquiring the old Unity Church and the Hamersley Building. By this time, Isidore Wise had become the largest individual property owner in the city's business section. He controlled almost all of a block of property bound by Main Street on the east, Church Street on the north and Pratt Street on the south. The exceptions were a building at the southwest corner of Main and Pratt and Christ Church Cathedral.

From 1918 to 1921, Wise erected several new buildings, all connected to the main store. One was a two-story rental property on Pratt Street, designed by Isaac A. Allen Jr., with space for specialty stores below and offices above. Next was an eight-story addition, at the rear of the main Wise, Smith & Company store. Recognizing that Pratt Street was "patronized by the better class of shoppers," Wise resisted offers to rent the Hamersley property to chain stores and determined to replace it with yet another addition, again

Wise, Smith & Company Building, Main Street, after the 1912 expansion. On the right is the Roberts Block. *Hartford Collection, Hartford History Center, Hartford Public Library.*

designed by Allen, that would be "the finest specialty shop on the street." Wise continued to acquire additional properties on Pratt Street later in the 1920s, including an 1888 building that had been home to the dry goods store of Jerome E. Sage.[141]

In 1929, the company again made substantial changes to its Main Street frontage. The Roberts Building and Opera House were demolished. In their

Wise, Smith & Company, circa 1929. The new section has been completed, and the earlier section is being altered to match it. On the right is the 1875 Miller Building. *Hartford Collection, Hartford History Center, Hartford Public Library.*

place rose a nine-story addition to the original store, designed in the art moderne style by Dennison & Hirons of New York. The following year, the façade of the 1897/1912 building was altered to match that of the new addition, creating an architecturally unified structure. In 1948, Isidore Wise sold the store to City Stores, Inc. When Wise, Smith & Company finally closed in 1954, control of the building was returned to the eighty-eight-year-old retired merchant. Wise passed away in 1956, and the following year, the interior of the building was completely remodeled to become the Hartford branch of E.J. Korvette, a national department store chain.[142] In the 1970s, the exterior was remodeled twice. On the second occasion, it became the American Airlines Building. Today, it is known as One American Plaza and houses shops and apartments.

The three department stores described in this chapter expanded in similar ways, but with some notable differences. All of them grew in increments, expanding as necessary by taking over adjacent property. G. Fox & Company experienced a devastating fire in 1917 but was then able to erect its impressive new store from scratch on a substantial scale. Sage-Allen built a series of interconnected structures but was not able to satisfactorily unify them until it acquired the building that housed Henry Kohn & Sons. When Sage-Allen eventually created a common façade for its buildings along Main Street, it was not a stylistically complete effort. The new front obscured part of the original Victorian architecture. Wise, Smith & Company acquired a series of buildings along Main Street and twice accommodated an earlier building into a new addition to create a streamlined façade.

For over half a century, Isidore Wise was in charge of Wise, Smith & Company. He rose from a cash boy to become Hartford's largest individual taxpayer. While his store was not as old and did not survive as long as G. Fox or Sage-Allen, it was in many ways a pioneer. This began with the novelty of a store that occupied seven floors and transported customers on an elevator. Wise himself felt that the other dry goods firms in the city had followed his store's lead in becoming department stores. The rapid pace of Wise, Smith & Company's development spurred a vitality that led to Hartford becoming a great retail center.[143] That era has now vanished, but the old façades of G. Fox, Sage-Allen and Wise, Smith & Company can still be admired today.

CHAPTER SIX

A FEW OF DOWNTOWN HARTFORD'S EARLY HOMESTEADS

The oldest surviving house in downtown Hartford is the Butler-McCook House on Main Street, built in 1782. Farther south on Main are the Ellery Hills House, dating to 1840, and the Henry Barnard House, built in 1807. These structures are isolated reminders of a time when numerous houses such as these could be found up and down Main and adjacent streets. These old residences, constructed during a period lasting from Hartford's earliest colonial days in the seventeenth century through the early nineteenth century, were eventually lost to downtown's development as a business center. Most were already gone over a century ago, when Samuel Taylor, a Hartford resident for most of his life, took photographs of numerous old homesteads that were soon to be destroyed. Through his efforts and those of others who recorded images and histories of Hartford's early homesteads, we can remember some of those that stood for centuries in the heart of downtown.

REVEREND THOMAS HOOKER'S HOUSE

An early attempt to represent a lost Hartford house can be found in John Warner Barber's *Connecticut Historical Collections*, published in 1836. On page forty-three is Barber's illustration of the house of Reverend Thomas Hooker (1586–1647), Hartford's first minister. The house, already lost by the early nineteenth century, had stood on School Street (now Arch Street),

John Warner Barber's illustration of Thomas Hooker's house. *Connecticut Historical Collections.*

just north of what would later be called the Park River. Barber, an artist and antiquarian, based his illustration of the Hooker House on a drawing, made just before the house was taken down. This drawing "was obtained from a gentleman now deceased, who devoted considerable time and attention to antiquarian researches in Hartford." The house appears to be typical of the more substantial "mansions" of the time: a two-story, wood-frame building with a single large chimney and a central projection. Barber explains that the projection was used by Reverend Hooker as his study.[141]

THE JOSEPH WHITING HOUSE

In the collections of the Connecticut Historical Society is a watercolor image depicting two houses. Attributed to George Francis, it was painted in the 1810s or 1820s. The two houses once stood on the east side of Main Street, in the block south of the Butler-McCook House. The scene presents the area before it became subject to extensive development. On the left is the Amos Bull House, a brick residence, built in 1788 and later moved to its current location on South Prospect Street. The house on the right was much older than its neighbor. It was named for Joseph Whiting (1645–1718), who served as treasurer of the Colony of Connecticut from 1679 until his death. Whiting purchased the property from Zachary Sandford in 1682. The house itself had been built even earlier, probably by Francis Barnard, who owned the land between 1650 and 1667. The residence's side, or gable end, faced Main Street. Its front faced south across a garden, toward what is now called Charter Oak Avenue. The house had a rear "lean-to" addition, built sometime before Whiting's death. Like other houses of this type, it had a steeply sloping roof in the rear, which gave it a traditional New England saltbox shape.

The Whiting House was photographed in the 1890s by Samuel Taylor. Like many of Hartford's other ancient houses, it had by then been converted to commercial use, with a redesigned entrance on Main Street. There were now additions on its north and south sides. One of these occupies the area that had been the front garden and blocks off the entrance that faces Charter Oak Avenue. The chimneys, visible in the earlier image, have been removed. During this period, the upper floor contained tenements while the first floor was home to Frederick E. Day's Saloon.[115]

In this altered form, the old Whiting House survived until May 1914, when contractor George B. Schwartz began to erect a six-story apartment building on the site where the house stood. By then, the saloon was operated by Ignatz J. Paredina, who would not allow this construction work to halt his business. He and William Hawksworth, the owner of the neighboring saloon on the corner, knew that any suspension of business would render their unexpired liquor licenses void. They would then have to begin again as new applicants. They wanted to avoid that situation because new licenses would not be granted under the current law due to the proximity of the South Congregational Church across the street. The persevering saloonkeepers kept their establishments open, even as their old homes were taken apart and a new building rose around them. On May 24, 1914, an article appeared in the *Hartford Courant* entitled "Saloon Airdomes Make Their Advent," which noted the removal of the saloon's roofs. Even as one of Hartford's oldest landmarks was gradually vanishing, "business was going on at the same old stand and men could last night quench their thirst at the bar and at the same time gaze up into the star-flecked sky."

On June 7, the *Courant* returned to the subject of two saloons ("Cramped Quarters for this Saloon"), explaining that workers, who had previously

The Joseph Whiting House (center) in its later days as Frederick E. Day's saloon. On the far left is part of the Amos Bull House. *Taylor Collection, State Archives, Connecticut State Library.*

put up a building within a building for Mr. Hawksworth, had finally removed the outer shell, "leaving a piano-box sort of structure," so tiny that "if one in the line before the bar relaxes and forgets to stand erect, the place immediately becomes crowded for the others." Under these cramped conditions, business could continue in the two saloons, while "during the working day the chant of a steam shovel in the rear furnishes a cabaret effect for those inside."

A number of other colonial houses managed to survive into the early years of the twentieth century. One was the Sheldon Woodbridge House on Governor Street. The house was widely believed to have been the home of Connecticut's second governor, Edward Hopkins, but was probably built in the later seventeenth century by Major James Richards.[116] At the corner of Grove and Prospect Streets was the 1750 house built by Dr. Roderick Morrison, which was moved farther south on Prospect in 1829. For a time, this had been the home of Thomas Green, who in 1764 founded the *Connecticut Courant.* Nearby, on Grove Street, stood a house built in 1778 for Barnabas Deane, a merchant and the brother of the Revolutionary War diplomat Silas Deane. It survived into the 1920s, when it was demolished to provide parking space for the Hartford Club.[117]

Six Central Row and the Hartford-Connecticut Trust Company Building as they appear today. *Author photo.*

Palace Theater and D'Esopo (aka Palace) Building, Main Street. *Postcard, courtesy of Tomas Nenortas.*

Hotel Heublein, HARTFORD, Conn.

Above: Façade of the First National Bank as integrated into State House Square. *Author photo*.

Opposite: Hotel Heublein, corner of Wells and Gold Streets. *Postcard, courtesy of Tomas Nenortas*.

Arch Street entrance to the Municipal Building. The lions once stood in front of the
Phoenix National Bank on Main Street. *Author photo.*

Main Street, 1907. *From left to right*: the Aetna (Fire) Insurance Company Building of 1905
and the Aetna Life Insurance Company Building (originally the home of the Charter Oak
Life Insurance Company). *Postcard, courtesy of Tomas Nenortas.*

Main Street, circa 1908. First section of the Travelers Insurance Building and the Universalist Church's building. *Postcard, courtesy of Tomas Nenortas.*

Connecticut Mutual Life Insurance Company Building after expansion, corner of Main and Pearl Streets. *Postcard, courtesy of Tomas Nenortas.*

Hartford Fire Insurance Company Building, after expansion, corner of Trumbull and Pearl Streets. *Postcard, courtesy of Tomas Nenortas.*

Pearl Street, looking east. *Author photo*.

Hartford National Bank Building, corner of Main and Asylum Streets. *Postcard, courtesy of Tomas Nenortas.*

YMCA Building of 1893 with 1914 addition. *Postcard, courtesy of Tomas Nenortas.*

YMCA Building from Bushnell Park. *Postcard, courtesy of Tomas Nenortas.*

Allyn House, corner of Trumbull and Asylum Streets. On the left is the 1915 Majestic Theater, which replaced Allyn Hall. *Postcard, courtesy of Tomas Nenortas.*

Main Street, 2004. Sage, Allen & Company Building as modified in the 1960s to present a uniform façade. To the left of Sage-Allen is the two-story structure that replaced the Ballerstein Building. Left of that is the 1876 Cheney Building, now called the Richardson Building. On the right is part of State House Square. The Sage-Allen Building has been greatly altered since this photo was taken. *Photograph by Trix Rosen ©2005.*

Hartford Life Insurance Company Building, corner of Asylum and Ann Streets, circa 1907. *Postcard, courtesy of Tomas Nenortas.*

Hotel Garde, Hartford, Conn.

The Garde Hotel, Hartford, Conn.

Postcards of the Hotel Garde, corner of Asylum and High Streets. *Courtesy of Tomas Nenortas.*

The Amos Bull House (left) and the Joseph Whiting House (right), circa 1810–29. Painting attributed to George Francis. *The Connecticut Historical Society, Hartford, Connecticut.*

The Lofts at Main and Temple, formerly Sage, Allen & Company. *Author photo.*

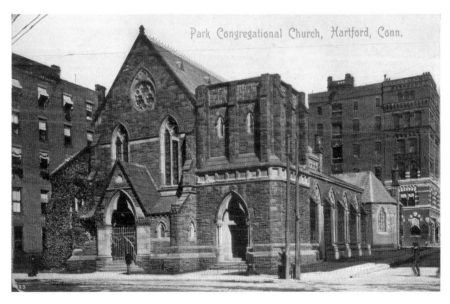

Park Congregational Church, corner of Asylum and High Streets. *Postcard, courtesy of Tomas Nenortas.*

St. John's Episcopal Church, Main Street. *Postcard, courtesy of Tomas Nenortas.*

TWO TALCOTT HOUSES

Two other early houses, ones that did not quite make it into the twentieth century, were located on Main Street, north of Church Street. One, at the southeast corner of Main and Talcott Streets, was built circa 1725 by Governor Joseph Talcott. The other, built in 1770 by the governor's son, Colonel Samuel Talcott, stood a little farther north on the other side of Main Street. By the 1890s, both had been converted to commercial use.

The first house to go was the younger of the two, the Samuel Talcott House at 459 Main Street. One contemporary lamented its destruction in an article entitled "An Old Mansion," which appeared in the *Courant* on May 27, 1898. The house, he wrote,

> is being ruthlessly torn down by workmen who have neither a thought for its own history nor for that of those who lived there over a century ago... Tomorrow it will have existence only in a pile of timbers and in a few months even they will be cleared away and a row of one-story stores will occupy the place.

The work of razing the historic structure brought to light a number of lost relics. An old hammer, probably used in building the house, was found, as well as an inkstand bearing the mark June 18, 1772. Discovered in the rafters was a wooden cane with a steel dagger concealed in the handle. The reporter speculated that a silver plate bearing the inscription "M.P." must have belonged to Colonel Matthew Talcott, Samuel Talcott's brother, who resided in Middletown. There was an old saying that "whenever Colonel Matthew Talcott went from Middletown to Hartford, as he crossed the Little Bridge he made all Hartford tremble, because he held so many mortgages there." In 1775, he was a member of the committee appointed to provide for the prisoners of war sent to Hartford from Fort Ticonderoga.[148]

The older Talcott House was built in 1725, or perhaps even earlier, by Samuel and Matthew's father, Governor Joseph Talcott. Born in 1669, he served as governor of Connecticut from 1724 until his death in 1741. In a letter to the *Hartford Courant*, published on July 27, 1900, and headlined "History of an Old House," Mary K. Talcott provides details about the governor's old homestead. It is said to have incorporated timbers from an even earlier house, built for the governor's grandfather, John Talcott. The house was later inherited by Samuel Talcott's daughter Mary and her husband, James Watson. In 1800, the couple sold it to the Reverend

Samuel Talcott House, Main Street. *Taylor Collection, State Archives, Connecticut State Library.*

Governor Joseph Talcott House, corner of Main and Talcott Streets. *Hartford Collection, Hartford History Center, Hartford Public Library.*

Joseph Steward, a minister and artist, whose Museum of Natural and Other Curiosities was located on the third floor of the Old State House. He soon moved the museum to the second floor of the Talcott House, where it remained until both he and his widow, Sarah Moseley Steward, had passed away. The collection then moved to the Central Row Building, across from the Old State House. Ownership of the Talcott House passed to Sarah's heirs, members of the Moseley family.

Until it was finally demolished in 1900, the house had long been a source of dispute between its owners and the City of Hartford. In 1761, Samuel Talcott had deeded the right of way through the property to create Talcott Street, which ran from the northeast corner of the house at Main Street eastward to Front Street. Difficulties would arise from the fact that part of the north side of the house extended beyond the building line into the new street. Part of the house was even removed to allow a way through, but even with this alteration, the house encroached on part of the street. In 1800, when James and Mary Watson sold the house to Reverend Steward, they also deeded to the city a piece of land five feet, four inches wide on the south side of Talcott Street, reserving the right for the house to overhang the street that distance for as long as it remained standing. Unable to force the removal of the house, the city council grappled on and off for years over the issue of what to do about this unusual corner. In order to provide room for a sidewalk, part of the rear section of the house was eventually removed along the basement level, but the upper floors still projected above the heads of passing pedestrians.

In 1899, Hamilton W. Conklin, agent for the house's owner, Edward S. Moseley of Newburyport, Massachusetts, leased the property to the dry goods firm of Simon Ragovin & Company. The new lessee planned to make substantial repairs, build a new brick addition and put in a large glass show window facing Main Street. The building inspector issued a permit but later revoked it. This denial was followed by a court injunction, which prevented any work from being done. These actions had been urged by the city attorney, who maintained that no improvements could be made that would prolong the building's natural existence. He feared that repairing the deteriorating building might void the city's claim to part of the land. Litigation commenced, and it was thought that the case would probably go to the state supreme court for a final decision, but a settlement was eventually reached. On June 1, 1900, Edward S. Moseley had died. Acting as agent for his heirs, Conklin proceeded to sign an agreement whereby the city would pay them $400 in return for dropping the suit. The old homestead was to be demolished. As the *Courant* observed, "The agreement is regarded as an excellent one for the City and a good piece of work by the city attorney."[149]

THE WADSWORTH HOUSES

Another notable old Hartford homestead that witnessed its share of stirring events stood on the present site of the Wadsworth Atheneum on Main Street. This was the home of Jeremiah Wadsworth (1743–1804). He was the son of Reverend Daniel Wadsworth, pastor of First Church, and Abigail Talcott, the daughter of Governor Joseph Talcott and sister of Matthew and Samuel Talcott. Beginning at the age of eighteen, Jeremiah worked for ten years on merchant ships owned by his uncle, Matthew Talcott of Middletown. During this time, he rose from common sailor to captain. Wadsworth then returned to the family homestead in Hartford and established himself as the city's wealthiest and most prominent citizen. In 1775, he was appointed commissary to the Patriot forces raised in Connecticut. From April 1778 to December 1779, he was commissary general to the Continental army. He then served with the French forces in America in the same capacity until the end of the Revolutionary War. After the war, Wadsworth was a member of the state convention that ratified the U.S. Constitution and served three terms in the U.S. House of Representatives.

In 1780, the French general Comte de Rochambeau arrived with his army in Newport to aid the American revolutionaries. He had his first conference with George Washington in the Hartford home of Jeremiah Wadsworth on September 20–21. The proceedings were cut short when word arrived of a British naval buildup off the coast of New York.[150]

A barn, believed to have been built around 1730 by Reverend Daniel Wadsworth, Jeremiah's father, was used to stable Washington's horse during his meeting with Rochambeau in 1780. This structure was razed in 1801 and rebuilt in a grand Palladian style to better match the Georgian refinement of Jeremiah Wadsworth's House.[151] The stable stood on the other side of what was later called Atheneum Street.

Prospect Street, which would soon become home to some of Hartford's most fashionable residences, was laid out in 1788 to the rear of Jeremiah Wadsworth's house. In 1798, Wadsworth built a house at Thirty-three Prospect Street and sold it to his son, Daniel Wadsworth, in 1803. He built another house for his daughter, who had married General Nathaniel Terry. This residence was located at Nineteen Prospect Street.

Talcott and Wadsworth Families

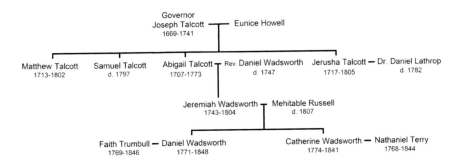

Family tree. *Created by the author.*

Daniel Wadsworth (1771–1848) inherited his father's wealth. An amateur artist and architect, he became a prominent patron of the arts. He supported the landscape painter Thomas Cole and later encouraged Cole to take on the Hartford-born painter Frederic Edwin Church as a student. Wadsworth created a lavish estate on Talcott Mountain, west of Hartford, which he named Monte Video. In the 1840s, Daniel Wadsworth created a public gallery as a culmination of his dedication to the arts. He generously donated the land where his father's house stood on Main Street for this purpose. The old house was moved to the corner of Buckingham and John Streets (it was eventually torn down in 1887). In 1844, the Wadsworth Atheneum opened on the house's former location. This institution, with its castle-like façade designed by Ithiel Town and Alexander Jackson Davis, survives today and is recognized as the oldest public art museum in the country.

A memoir by Lydia Huntley Sigourney (1791–1865) provides a glimpse of what life was like at the Wadsworth family homes at the start of the nineteenth century. Later a well-known poet, Lydia Huntley grew up in Norwich, Connecticut. Her father, Ezekiel Huntley, worked as a gardener for Mrs. Jerusha Talcott Lathrop. Lydia Huntley grew very close to Mrs. Lathrop, a widow, who was the daughter of Governor Joseph Talcott and the aunt of Jeremiah Wadsworth. In 1805, after the death of Mrs. Lathrop, the grieving Huntley was sent on a trip to Hartford to visit Mrs. Jeremiah Wadsworth. Her husband had passed away the year before, but Mrs. Wadsworth continued to reside in the house on Main Street with two of her late husband's elderly sisters.

Jeremiah Wadsworth House. Originally on Main Street, later moved to John Street. *Taylor Collection, State Archives, Connecticut State Library.*

Huntley was fatigued by her long journey, which had included a crossing of the Connecticut River from East Hartford on a large flat-bottomed boat. In her memoir, she recalled that she had retired to bed early that night:

> *As I lay ruminating, and reviewing the scenes of the day, I heard a pleasant sound—the bells from the steeples of the North and South churches ringing for the hour of nine. They strike alternately two strokes, each waiting for the other, then, joining, tell with one voice the day of the month—in unison. One has a deep, heavy tone, the other a melodious one; and their concord is like that of bass and treble in perfect harmony. I remembered that this had been described to me of old, by my loved and departed friend.*

The young Lydia long remembered the refinement of life at the Wadsworth House, noting that the "comfort of this interesting and dignified family was promoted by a band of well-trained and trustworthy servants, a cook, chambermaid, and waiter, gardener, and coachman." Some of these servants may have been slaves or former slaves. The Wadsworth House was "old-fashioned but commodious." Built of wood, it *had a pleasant vine-covered piazza, with a southern exposure, and had been enlarged in the rear by a range of chambers resting on heavy stone columns, which by moonlight had a picturesque effect. Connected with the court was a large garden, filled with luxuriant fruit-trees, a variety of herbs which were thought to have affinity with health, and the largest and most fragrant damask-rose bushes. I speak more particularly of these premises because they are now occupied by the fine edifice of granite known as the "Wadsworth Athenaeum," and their original aspect will soon have faded from the memory of the living.*

Huntley also visited the two nearby "elegant mansions" that Jeremiah Wadsworth had built for his children on Prospect Street. From the father's house, the home of the son "was accessible through their united grounds." Daniel Wadsworth and his wife, Faith Trumbull, daughter of Governor Jonathan Trumbull, kept a fine household:

Their spacious apartments displayed that exquisite taste, and liberal patronage of the fine arts, that ever distinguished the master of the mansion. There I first enjoyed the luxury of studying fine pictures; and in this abode, and also in that of his mother, revelled [sic] in the delights of a large and select library.

Next door was the house Jeremiah built for his daughter, Catharine Wadsworth Terry,

a lady of fair and sweetly expressive countenance and commanding presence, and who, in many noble traits of character, was said to bear resemblance to him. Her husband, General Nathaniel Terry, stood high in the legal profession, possessed fine talents, a finished education, and was in manners a perfect gentleman of the old school. Surrounded by a large family of uncommonly beautiful and promising children, these three households formed a delightful circle, often meeting in social festivals, and comprising a remarkable range and variety of age, accomplishments, and wisdom.[152]

Lydia Huntley returned to Norwich, and in 1811 she started a school for girls. Three years later, under the patronage of Daniel Wadsworth, she set up a similar school in Hartford. Wadsworth also helped her to publish her first work, *Moral Pieces in Prose and Verse*, in 1815. Huntley married Charles Sigourney, a wealthy widower, and lived the rest of her life in Hartford.

Daniel Wadsworth House, Prospect Street. *Taylor Collection, State Archives, Connecticut State Library.*

Nathaniel and Catharine Wadsworth Terry House, later the residence of Austin C. Dunham, Prospect Street. *Taylor Collection, State Archives, Connecticut State Library.*

In 1835, Austin Dunham came to Hartford and soon established himself as a prosperous wool merchant. After residing for a time on Front Street, he moved his family to Prospect Street. His son, Austin C. Dunham, notes in his *Reminiscences* that there were two houses on Prospect, built by Jeremiah Wadsworth:

> *The gardens of these two houses lay in front of them to the east and ran down in terraces as far as Front street. Later two of the Watkinson brothers also built on this street, and one or two other straggling houses followed. My father bought the south garden which belonged to one of the Wadsworth houses which had been occupied by his son-in-law, General Terry, and built there, on the east side of the street, the first residence owned by him in Hartford.* [153]

By that time, the Terry House was the residence of Dr. Henry Grant, but it was eventually acquired by Austin Dunham, who died in 1877. The house passed to his children, but was eventually torn down around 1907 to make way for the construction of the Morgan Memorial Building of the Wadsworth Atheneum. The Daniel Wadsworth House lasted longer. In the mid-nineteenth century it was owned by William H. Imlay, Hartford's leading merchant. For a time it was occupied by the Hartford Theological Seminary, and in 1881, it was remodeled by architect S.W. Lincoln to serve as the new home of the Hartford Club. Founded in 1873, the club had had several earlier homes on Prospect Street. Alterations to the Wadsworth House included making space for a billiard room and constructing a new veranda on the south side of the house. The Hartford Club, which leased the house from the Wadsworth Atheneum, moved to a new building on Prospect Street in 1904. The Atheneum then converted the house for its own use. The Hartford Public Library was located in the Atheneum Building at the time and was in need of more space. The first floor of the house became the library's Children's Branch while the upper floor became an annex gallery for the Atheneum. The former residence of Daniel Wadsworth was eventually torn down in 1932 to make way for the Atheneum's Avery Memorial wing. [154]

By the early 1950s, the Wadsworth houses had vanished, but the old stable of the original house remained. It was owned by the Hartford Public Library, which planned to sell the land and use the funds to defray the costs of constructing a new library on Main Street. Infested with termites and condemned as a hazard by the Hartford fire marshal, the stable was slated to be taken down in 1952. Action to save the building was led by Katherine

Seymour Day, a grandniece of Harriet Beecher Stowe and a descendant of Thomas Hooker. Day was devoted to historic preservation and resided in the Harriet Beecher Stowe House on Forrest Street. Day formed a group called the Friends of Hartford, which raised funds to move the stable to Lebanon, Connecticut. It was restored in 1954 and presented to the Connecticut Daughters of the American Revolution.[155] Today, it is open to the public as a museum. The Wadsworth houses, which once stood near the stable in Hartford, have long since vanished, but Daniel Wadsworth's devotion to the arts continues in the form of the museum he founded.

CHAPTER SEVEN

CONTINUITY AND CHANGE IN DOWNTOWN'S CONGREGATIONAL CHURCHES

Long before the era of modern skyscrapers, church steeples dominated the skyline of Hartford. Early nineteenth-century illustrations of the city, such as the one by John Warner that appears in his classic 1836 volume, *Connecticut Historical Collections*, display the many spires towering over neighboring buildings. A lithographic print published in 1849 called *A View of Hartford from the Deaf and Dumb Asylum* shows no fewer than twelve churches on or near Main Street, only a few of which survive today. A number of churches constructed in the nineteenth century survived into the early twentieth century. Most were eventually torn down as their congregations followed the movement of population to newer neighborhoods, often on the edge of the developing city. The many lost churches of downtown Hartford succumbed to the pressures of commercial development and changing demographics.

Hartford's past and present churches reflect the evolving styles and tastes of earlier eras. The earliest New England church buildings were simple wooden structures, often resembling oversized houses. In the eighteenth century, church architecture was dominated by the Georgian style. These churches featured soaring steeples and ornamentation derived from the architecture of classical Greece and Rome. After the American Revolution, this classicism, with extensive use of columns and formal pediments, became even more ornately detailed in what is known as the Federal style. By the second quarter of the nineteenth century, the Greek revival style, with squared steeples and less elaborate designs that were more precisely based

"View of Hartford From the Eastern Bank of the Connecticut River," by John Warner Barber. *Connecticut Historical Collections.*

on the original proportions of ancient Greek temples, came to dominate church architecture.

In the middle and later years of the nineteenth century, Hartford churches were commonly built in romantic and picturesque styles that looked back to the medieval era. In Europe, the Romanesque architecture of the eleventh and twelfth centuries had been followed by the Gothic architecture of the high Middle Ages. Romanesque revival churches featured round-arched doors and windows with stringcourses and corbel tables. Gothic revival churches, with their distinctive pointed arches, were initially built by Episcopal and Catholic parishes to distinguish themselves from the dominant New England Congregationalists, but the style soon became popular with all denominations. Portland, Connecticut, was famed for its brownstone quarries, which supplied the stone for Hartford's grandest Romanesque and Gothic churches.

Hartford's vanished houses of worship are worth recalling because they stood for decades as fixtures of the streetscape of Hartford, serving generations of churchgoers. They also provided pulpits for some of the most celebrated clergymen of their time.

Hartford was founded in the 1630s by Puritan Congregationalists from England. One of their first priorities, after constructing their own dwellings, was to build a meetinghouse. They did not consider this building to be a church. The term church referred instead to the body of members who made up the congregation. The meetinghouse was the place where the congregation met, and in the days before the separation of church and state, it was also the place where residents conducted town business. As the Congregational Church was the officially established church in Connecticut, the residents of each town were obligated to attend Sunday services and pay taxes to support their local Congregational church or else prove that they were attending and supporting one of the dissenting churches. It is therefore not surprising that the meetinghouses built in Hartford in the colonial period were all Congregational. However, in the years after the Revolutionary War, Episcopalians and Baptists began to construct their own church buildings in the city. These were followed in the early nineteenth century by churches of other denominations. The Connecticut constitution of 1818 officially disestablished the Congregational Church. Although no longer supported by the state, Congregational churches continued to flourish. New congregations were established downtown in the early to mid-nineteenth century, joining those with histories dating back to colonial times.

EARLY CONGREGATIONAL MEETINGHOUSES

Two Congregational meetinghouses still stand as important landmarks on Main Street in Hartford. The First Church of Christ in Hartford, called Center Church, was built in 1807. Farther south is the Second Church of Christ, called South Church, built in 1827. These two Federal-style buildings were preceded by earlier structures that are now lost. The first meetinghouse in Hartford was built in 1636. Intended as a temporary structure, it was most likely built of logs. Around 1640, it was given to the community's minister, the Reverend Thomas Hooker, to use as a barn. The next meetinghouse, begun in 1638, was a plain, square, wooden building with a pyramidal hip roof, topped by a small cupola, referred to as a "tower and turret." An enclosed porch covered the front doorway. As the population increased, galleries were added inside to provide additional space. Both of these early buildings were located on sections of Meeting House Yard, an area surrounding the spot where the Old State House stands today. The first meetinghouse was in the vicinity of Central Row while the second was on the eastern end of the yard, where today State Street ends.[156]

Doctrinal issues after the death of Thomas Hooker led to division in the church and the establishment of the Second Church of Christ in Hartford

The Meeting House of 1638. The Colonial History of Hartford, *by William DeLoss Love.*

in 1670. This event also reflected other divisions in the town's early history between residents dwelling north and south of what would later be called the Park River. The new south congregation's first meetinghouse, erected at the corner of what are now Main and Sheldon Streets just south of the river, probably resembled the First Church's wooden meetinghouse of the time. The construction of this second meetinghouse in Hartford relieved overcrowding in the older building for a time, but in 1737, the First Church finally vacated its 1638 meetinghouse, which was soon torn down. In 1739, the congregation moved into a third meetinghouse. Built of wood, it stood on the southeast corner of the burying ground, along what is now Main Street.[157] A later pastor, Reverend George Leon Walker described the meetinghouse in a history of the church:

> *The house stood sidewise to the street, its steeple on the north end. There was a door at the south end, another on the east side, and another under the steeple on the north. The pulpit was on the west side, and over it a sounding-board, and behind it a curtain.*[158]

Ten years later, the Second Church also decided to build a new meetinghouse. It stood where Buckingham Street intersects with Main Street, in the middle of the road itself. By the 1820s, this unusual location had become inconvenient, and the building was regarded as an obstacle to traffic. On December 2, 1754, the first sermon in the building was given by Reverend George Whitefield (1714–70), the legendary English preacher and leader of the First Great Awakening.[159] Reverend Edwin Pond Parker, who was the minister of South Church from 1860 to 1912, writes in his 1892 history of the church that

> *this meeting-house is distinctly remembered by several persons now residing in Hartford, some of whom attended worship there as boys and girls. It was a wooden structure, and, like that of the First Church, stood sidewise to Main Street, with an entrance on the east side and also at either end. There was a porch under the steeple at the north end. On the west side stood a structure for housing a rude apparatus for use in case of fires. Within were galleries, square pews, and a pulpit on the west side overhung by a sounding-board.*[160]

Both the 1739 First Church and the 1754 Second Church were replaced in the early nineteenth century by the buildings that continue to serve the respective congregations of Center Church and South Church today.

NORTH CONGREGATIONAL CHURCH AND PARK CONGREGATIONAL CHURCH

In 1824, the First and Second Congregational Churches were joined by the Third Congregational Church, also called North Church. The rapidly increasing membership of Center Church during the ministry of Reverend Joel Hawes (1818–67) had led to overcrowding and the need to start a new church.[161] North Congregational Church's meetinghouse was erected at the intersection of Main, Village and Morgan Streets, north of where the G. Fox building was later built. Like Center Church (1807) and South Church (1827), it was a classically inspired building with a pedimented front façade and an elaborate steeple. In the 1830s, galleries were added at the rear inside the building, and a few years later, the interior was completely reconstructed with galleries on the sides.[162] The very first sermon in the new church was preached by a notable minister, Reverend Lyman Beecher, the father of author Harriet Beecher Stowe.[163]

North Church's third pastor, Reverend Horace Bushnell (1802–1876), was Hartford's most famous and influential minister. He served from 1833 until he resigned in 1859 due to poor health. A controversial and opinionated theologian, Reverend Bushnell was also a key civic leader who pushed for the creation of the park that now bears his name. He continued to live in Hartford until his death in 1876 and maintained a strong interest in the church. After the Civil War, when North Church was planning to move away from Main Street, it is said that Dr. Bushnell's advice was, "Do not go north, go west." He suggested their new location, at the northwest corner of Asylum and High Streets, opposite the north end of Bushnell Park.[164]

With its congregation moving west, the old church was sold in 1866 to William Toohy and Soloman Cohn, who transformed the building into a bazaar for stores. An article in the *Hartford Courant* on September 18, 1866, related that

> *a large crowd was gathered on Main street, about 6 o'clock last evening, to witness the pulling down of a portion of the old North Church steeple. About twenty feet of the steeple had been partially sawed off, when a rope was hitched to it near the top, and a large number of persons, with our friend Toohy at the head, took hold of the rope and pulled. The steeple soon came down with a loud crash, amid the cheers of the crowd. The remainder of the steeple will probably be taken down in pieces from the inside.*[165]

The church had chosen to move due to the encroachment of businesses on Main Street and the large number of other churches in the vicinity. The cornerstone of their new building, to be known as the Park Congregational Church, was laid on June 7, 1866, and the edifice was dedicated on March 29, 1867. A Gothic structure built of Portland brownstone, it had a short tower on its southeast corner, intended to be the base of a tall spire that was never built.

A reporter for the *Hartford Courant*, while admiring the new church's architecture, noted the doubts that some held concerning its location:

> *It was feared at first that the building would not show to advantage on the low and somewhat crowded lot, on which it was to be built. It is even now a question whether some better site might not have been selected, yet an edifice which commands the range of Washington street, Elm street, Trinity*

Row, and the whole section of the Park intervening, cannot be said to be hidden or even inconspicuous. Twenty years from this time there will be few more desirable fronts in the city than those on the Park.

A harsher judgment was expressed by another *Courant* writer in 1921. The recent announcement that the church had finally been sold, the writer explains, "marks the end of an experiment that failed." When built, "the situation facing Bushnell Park seemed wisely selected, and the spot was beginning to be central at that time, but the church never seemed to flourish."[166]

Although its membership had not grown to the extent originally anticipated, it had remained a strong church. For many years, its pastor was the distinguished minister Reverend Nathaniel Judson Burton. He came to Hartford in 1857 to become minister of the Fourth Congregational Church but moved to Park Church in 1870, serving until his death in 1887. For a time, Reverend Burton resided on Forest Street, in the Hartford neighborhood of Nook Farm. Among his neighbors was the lawyer John Hooker,[167] a notable parishioner of Park Church, whose sister-in-law, Harriet Beecher Stowe, also lived on Forest Street.

In 1914, Park Church's congregation moved even farther west, to merge with the Farmington Avenue Congregational Church. On Sunday, April 19, 1914, the last services were held in the old church. Many congregants lingered for a while in their pews with bowed heads, unwilling to depart.[168] The building, however, did continue as a house of worship, being rented to the Second Church of Christ, Scientist until its sale in 1921. The building was eventually demolished in 1925 to make way for the new building of the Capitol National Bank and Trust, which is still standing today.

FOURTH CONGREGATIONAL CHURCH

Until the early twentieth century, churches commonly rented pews as a way to raise income. This practice resulted in the wealthy having the best seats, reflecting their social status. It also led to overcrowding, as the remaining free space was not always sufficient for those who wanted to attend services. In the mid-nineteenth century, controversy over the renting of pews led to the creation of "free churches" in many cities. Hartford's Free Church, which dispensed with pew rental, was established in 1832, although within a few years financial pressure forced the church to adopt the practice. It then became known as the Fourth Congregational Church of Hartford.[169] By that time, the church had already built its meetinghouse on Main Street, north of Center Church and south of North Church. In 1850, the church moved to a new and much larger building located farther along Main Street, after it takes a sharp turn to the northwest.

The former Fourth Congregational Church Building continued for almost another fifty years as a theater with shops in front, known as the Melodeon. The *Hartford Courant* noted in November 1851 that the building had been "fitted up in good order expressly for lectures and concerts; when finished, it will be a very pleasant place for such purposes. The house is large and will accommodate a large audience with good seats."[170] Not everyone was pleased with the building's transition from sacred to secular. On May 24, 1855, the *Courant* printed the following rant:

> *I don't know that I clearly understand how the term nuisance should be applied, if it does not describe such a piece of work as the ringing of that Melodeon bell at 6 o'clock, mornings. Is it to be tolerated? by what authority is it done? It must be pleasant for the neighbors, especially after sleepless nights! The whole manner of proceedings there, just now, is peculiar—but not to be wondered at perhaps. For it is only the working out of the original idea started when places of worship began to be decorated with dry goods signs. Now, we have profane advertisements, and what next, no one knows. It's all of a piece.*[171]

The Melodeon was torn down in 1897 to make way for the construction of the new Wise, Smith & Company department store. The new home of the Fourth Congregational Church was designed by Sidney Mason Stone of New Haven and was modeled, at the request of the congregation's building committee, on that city's Center Church on the Green. The result was a fine classical edifice, featuring a pedimented front porch with six Corinthian columns and a spire, varied with superimposed orders.[172] The *Courant* noted, on April 8, 1850, that "there is but one opinion expressed with reference to the new edifice, that it is uncommonly chaste and beautiful in its design and convenient in its arrangement." The *Courant* reporter continued to describe the inside of the building:

> *The walls and ceiling have been painted in fresco by Italian artists, with a perfection of perspective and a warmth yet pleasantness of color which it*

would be difficult to surpass, and which has been viewed with delight by our most competent judges. There is nothing in the city comparable with it, and before long the other churches will probably be similarly adorned.[173]

At the time the new building opened, the Fourth Church's pastor was William Weston Patton, who served from 1846 to 1857. He was an outspoken abolitionist who later became the president of Howard University, and during his tenure, the church became identified with the antislavery movement. Membership declined after the Civil War but revived in the 1880s. By 1913, the church had again decided to move, hiring the firm of Davis & Brooks to design a new church at Albany Avenue and Vine Street. As architect W.F. Brooks explained in a 1920 article, "By 1913 its congregation lived far to the northwest, and the encroachment of business had made its dignified porch and spire seem incongruous, but had increased the value of its real estate so that it could afford to move."[174] The *Courant* noted that

although the old field of the church is to be abandoned, church-officials believe there is a much wider chance for growth in the new location... This move is only following out the present tendencies of the downtown church to remove to the suburbs where a better opportunity for service is presented.[175]

Rather than completely abandoning the old church on Main Street, Brooks and Davis sought to preserve part of the old edifice. Brooks explains:

These architects explained the value, historic, sentimental, and real, of the easily removable porch and handsome spire for so many years one of the landmarks of Hartford, and that with these as the dominant adornment they would design a modern auditorium in keeping, agreeing thus to produce far richer and more important results than the money at hand could produce in new work.[176]

Through this early example of historic preservation, the steeple and porch of the 1850 church were transferred to the new church, which was dedicated in 1914. Part of what remained of the old church was incorporated into the Grand Theater, which later became the New Parsons Theater and was eventually demolished in 1960 to make way for Interstate 84.[177] Fourth Congregational Church continued for many decades in its new home. It merged in 1953 with Windsor Avenue Congregational Church to form

Horace Bushnell Congregational Church, which occupied the building into the twenty-first century. The historic church is now home to Liberty Christian Center International.

PEARL STREET CONGREGATIONAL CHURCH

In 1852, the four Congregational churches on Main Street were joined by a fifth, located on Pearl Street, just a few steps from Main. At the laying of the cornerstone of the Pearl Street Congregational Church on August 2, 1851, Reverend William Turner explained the need for the new church:

Most, if not all, the places of worship in this city are well filled on the Sabbath; and in some of them it has for a long time been difficult for all who have desired it to obtain seats. It is almost twenty years since a Congregational society has been formed in this town; and within that time our population has nearly doubled. Very few places in the Union are better supplied with the means of grace and with commodious houses of worship than Hartford. And yet we have a large number of residents who are not connected with any religious society and who seldom are seen in any place of worship on the Sabbath. The desire that all might be supplied with the means of grace and the hope that more might be induced to attend upon them by the opening of a new church, were leading motives in the present enterprise.[178]

A central downtown location on Pearl Street had been chosen for the new edifice, which was designed by the noted architect Minard Lafever of New York and constructed of Portland brownstone by Hartford builder Noah Wheaton.[179] The *Hartford Courant* described the building:

The Pearl Street Church, which is now completed, ranks high among the finest specimens of architecture in New England. Its style and finish is of the Romanesque…The building stands with its side to the Street, and is entered on the side. The main entrance is through the tower into the vestibule, which is very spacious…From the vestibule, you enter the audience room to the right…This room is finished with graceful Corinthian columns and capitals of beautiful proportions. The ceiling is very elaborate, being constructed with groined arches and pannel work [sic], with rich

Pearl Street Congregational
Church. *A Half-Century
History of the Farmington Avenue
Congregational Church.*

117

ornamental mouldings. Its beams spring over the nave, and rest on richly carved trusses…The ceiling is colored in parti-colors of an ultra-marine blue, and is so shaded in its several parts as to make it pleasing to the eye.

The system for supplying gaslight also attracted the writer's attention:

The arrangements for lighting with gas are of a novel style, the pipes being inside of the columns and no part of the fixtures visible to the eye but the burners, which appear just above the capitals of the columns. There are four burners to each capital, and the issuing light has a pleasing effect.[180]

When the Pearl Street Congregational Church was completed, there were still a number of residences in the immediate vicinity. By the 1890s, Pearl Street had been transformed into a business area of banks and insurance companies. In 1897, the church decided to sell its building and construct a new one on Farmington Avenue. The *Courant* reported on June 26, 1897, that

a prominent member of the church said last night that the society had for a long time felt the need of moving to a more western part of the city. Those who attend the services for the most part live a considerable distance away and besides there are more church-goers on Asylum and Farmington avenues than the churches in that vicinity can accommodate.[181]

Pearl Street Congregational Church was vacated in 1899 and torn down to make way for an extension of the Connecticut Mutual Life Insurance Company's headquarters. For almost a half century prior to its demolition, the church's spire had been a distinctive Hartford landmark, recognized as perhaps the finest steeple in the city. Because of the expense, it was originally to be constructed of wood, but a special subscription by eight individuals had made it possible to construct it of stone.[182] It had suffered damage when on "December 10, 1878, a southeast gale blew off the finial with other stones from the spire sending them through the roof into the lecture room and vestibule."[183] The spire was repaired the following year at a considerable cost.[184] Twenty years later, the steeple was taken down, although one "well known" member of the church, quoted in the *Courant*, thought that it could have been saved, saying, "It would be more of an ornament to the city than the Keney Memorial tower."[185] The paper lamented the spire's impending destruction:

The determination of the Connecticut Mutual to take down the Pearl street Church receives general endorsement. As a business proposition, nothing else could be done. But the change will destroy one of the beauties of Hartford architecture. The delicate and finely proportioned spire has long been admired. Senator Hawley, who has had the good fortune to occupy in his life a number of high positions, once sat for a few moments upon the very capstone, which is at the top of that needlelike structure! It is about 212 feet from the ground, a dizzying height. The general, however, took the precaution to sit on the stone before it was raised to its place on the spire and when it was lying on the ground. He said he wanted to be able to point to it and say he had sat upon it.[186]

The removal of that heavy capstone, together with the rest of the steeple, would present a considerable challenge for William F. O'Neil, the contractor hired to demolish the church. The walls were straightforward enough: they were pulled down with the help of a steam engine. To tackle the steeple, O'Neil called upon John Kiffe, a painter by trade, who also specialized in working on church steeples and had earned the nickname "Steeple Jack." The upper part of the steeple was solid masonry, which made it impossible to take down from inside. Going up on the inside as far as he could, Kiffe made an opening to the exterior at a point twenty-five feet below the capstone. He then worked his way up the outside of the steeple by means of "pegging and loops of rope." At first, he planned to loosen the capstone and then throw it down, doing the same with the remaining stones until the spire was demolished. The capstone turned out to be much heavier than anticipated.

Afraid that its fall would cause damage to surrounding buildings, another plan was adopted.[187] An article in the *Connecticut Magazine* describes the results:

The spire was two hundred and twelve feet in height and the falling section forty feet. A tier of stones on the northeast side was removed and replaced by a jack and block, followed by the removal of one-half the diameter of the spire at the base of the block. A heavy rope and pulley had been attached to the top and when the block was blown out by dynamite, the upper shaft bowed gracefully to earth, presenting one of the grandest spectacles, witnessed by thousands of people who had been watching and waiting for the culmination of this event for the previous ten hours.[188]

Falling section of the steeple of Pearl Street Church, Hartford, August 26, 1899. Photograph by Dr. Joseph E. Root. *The Connecticut Historical Society, Hartford, Connecticut.*

The *Hartford Times* reported that

> *Dr. Joseph E. Root was one of the most interested of the observers, as he was having plans made for photographing the spire as it fell, taking sketches by the instantaneous process. The cameras for this purpose were placed on the roof of the Phoenix Life Insurance Company's building, thereby securing the best of positions for the undertaking.*[189]

The Pearl Street Church's former congregation had its first service in its new building on September 10, 1899. Designed by Ernest Flagg, it was originally called the Farmington Avenue Congregational Church until it merged with Park Church in 1914. The newly united church took the name Immanuel Congregational Church and continues to occupy the same building on Farmington Avenue today.

TALCOTT STREET CONGREGATIONAL CHURCH

Extending beyond Main Street to the Connecticut River, Hartford's East Side was home to generations of immigrants from Europe and to an early community of African Americans. This neighborhood was eliminated in the mid-twentieth century to make way for Constitution Plaza. A lone church building from the old East Side survives on Market Street. Built as a mission to the area's immigrants, it was originally St. Paul's Episcopal Church but later became the German Lutheran Church of the Reformation and then St. Anthony's Catholic Church. The building survives today as offices of Catholic Charities. Just half a block away once stood another church with an important history.

The origins of the Talcott Street Congregational Church go back to 1819, when African Americans, tired of being relegated to seats in the galleries or in the rear of the city's churches, began holding their own religious services. In 1826, the pioneering African Religious Society built a Federal-style stone and brick church on Talcott Street, at the corner of Market Street. In 1833, the church joined the Congregational denomination. For a time, it was called the First Hartford Colored Congregational Church, later the Fifth Congregational Church and, from 1860, the Talcott Street Congregational Church. The church became a center for abolitionism and social activism.

In its basement was a district school for African American children, who at the time were not admitted to the public schools.[190] Prominent among the church's ministers in the 1840s was the Reverend James W.C. Pennington (1809–1870), a fugitive slave from Maryland who became a leading African American preacher, orator and abolitionist leader. Reverend Pennington was in danger of being dragged back to slavery until John Hooker, an abolitionist lawyer who was the brother-in-law of Harriet Beecher Stowe, purchased his freedom from the estate of his former owner.

In 1901, Reverend Robert F. Wheeler gave a historical sermon as part of the celebration of the seventy-fifth anniversary of the building of the Talcott Street Congregational Church. The pastor noted that

> *our Church became a center for reform work, an attractive point for kindred spirits, an opportunity for concentration and co-operation in the creation of public sentiment in the anti-slavery cause. More than once the building and the people within its hollowed walls have been assaulted and maltreated because of their devotion to liberty. In October, 1831, a serious riot developed here. "Certain lewd-fellows of the baser sort," stormed the building, defaced the walls, broke in some of the windows and drove away the congregation of worshipers. If the old building could speak it would say with the Apostle, "Henceforth let no man trouble me for I bear in my body the marks of the Lord Jesus."[191]*

Just a few years later, on March 25, 1906, Reverend Wheeler delivered another historical sermon, this time a farewell sermon to the historic church. He explained the need for a new building: "The character and materials of the original construction of this building and its constant use for nearly eighty years have reduced it to such a state of dilapidation as to render it practically uninhabitable and beyond the point of successful repairs."[192]

The old church was torn down, and the cornerstone of a new one, to be built on the same site, was laid on May 13, 1906. The new church, a brick structure in the Romanesque style with a short tower on its southeast corner, was designed by George H. Gilbert of Hartford. Sunday school and meeting rooms were on the first floor while on the upper floor were the audience room, choir gallery and a small assembly hall. The *Hartford Courant* reported that

> *the members consider the building somewhat in the light of a monument in commemoration of the noble and heroic souls who in the days of trial gallantly espoused the cause of the weak and oppressed, also as a reminder*

to this and succeeding generations of the patriotism believed and taught in it
and exemplified by the thirty-two men who went forth from the congregation
to the war for the union.[193]

In 1953, the Talcott Street Congregational Church merged with Mother Bethel Methodist Church to form the new Faith Congregational Church. By that time, its parishioners no longer lived in the neighborhood around Talcott Street, so the church decided to move into the vacated Windsor Avenue Congregational Church in Hartford's Clay Arsenal neighborhood. The old church on Talcott Street was soon torn down, but its cornerstone was preserved and placed in storage. In 1976, to celebrate the 150th anniversary of the building of the original Talcott Street Congregational Church, the old cornerstone was placed in the front wall of Faith Church.[194]

WARBURTON CHAPEL

Another landmark of Congregationalism on the East Side was the Warburton Chapel, which stood at Sixty-one Temple Street. Its origins went back to a Sunday school started in 1851 as a mission chapel. Known as the Union Sabbath School (under the oversight of Center Church), it occupied different quarters in the city until Mary A. Warburton endowed a permanent home for the school on Temple Street in memory of her husband, John Warburton. The Warburton Chapel, a Romanesque building with an impressive steeple on its northwest corner, was dedicated on June 28, 1866. The following day, the *Hartford Courant*, praised the new building as "conveniently and tastefully arranged" and singled out its architect, James Jordan, for personally superintending its construction and completing it within the allotted budget.[195]

The school grew rapidly and soon had to be expanded with the construction of a new primary room in 1873, the gift of Mrs. Charles Hosmer. On May 28, 1916, an article in the *Courant* noted that the still flourishing chapel would soon be celebrating the sixty-fifth anniversary of the founding of the original Sunday school. The article described the ongoing work of the city's oldest mission chapel, which had adapted to changing educational methods:

The purpose of the work being done by nearly forty teachers at the chapel
is to extend a Christian influence; to prepare the young children of the

East Side who attend its classes for citizenship and to make the girls more proficient in house-keeping and domestic arts, for which purpose classes in cooking, sewing and dressmaking are held, each of which is filled with eager "young mothers" who take great interest in the work. Industrial classes for boys are held several days each week and useful knowledge, such as banking and debating, are taught. A fine opportunity to engage in athletics of all kinds is given by the new gymnasium at the chapel. Religious instruction is given on Sunday only. [196]

By 1916, the neighborhood around the Warburton Chapel was primarily Italian, and the building also served as the home of the First Italian Congregational Church. Members of this congregation later moved to other Congregational churches in the city. In its final years, the chapel was the Casa Andrea of St. Anthony's Catholic Church. The chapel was demolished in 1960 to clear space for the building of Constitution Plaza, but proceeds from the sale of the building were used to help build the Warburton Community Church, an interracial church that is still in existence at 420 Brookfield Street, off Flatbush Avenue. [197]

CHAPTER EIGHT

PROLIFERATION OF DOWNTOWN CHURCHES

This chapter looks at Downtown Hartford's lost Episcopal, Catholic, Baptist, Methodist, Unitarian and Universalist church buildings. Like the city's Congregational churches, these denominations moved to new houses of worship in response to religious revival and changing demographics.

THE BUILDING THAT WAS HARTFORD'S FIRST EPISCOPAL AND FIRST CATHOLIC CHURCH

In the eighteenth century, Episcopalians faced many obstacles when they sought to build their own church in town. Congregationalists viewed them with suspicion as adherents of the Church of England. This was especially the case during the American Revolution, when many Episcopalians were Loyalists and their clergy opposed the rebellion. Although Episcopalians in Hartford had acquired land for a church in 1762, economic depression, legal squabbles and local resistance hindered construction. Christ Church was finally opened in 1795 at the northeast corner of what are now Main and Church Streets.[198] Built of wood, it "had a steeple adorned with four urns and surmounted with a spire." The church had round arched windows and "but one doorway, which was in the centre of the steeple, and this was ornamented with some carved work." Like Center Church, Christ Church had a governor's pew, covered by a canopy. There would be no Episcopalian

governor in office to occupy it until Jonathan Ingersoll was elected deputy governor in 1816.[199]

As the parish grew, Christ Church's old square pews were replaced with slips to accommodate more parishioners, but soon, even more space was required. In 1825, the parish began planning the construction of a new and larger church. Reverend Nathaniel S. Wheaton, rector of Christ Church, had traveled to England in 1824 to collect books for the new Washington (now Trinity) College. While there, he had observed the Gothic architecture of Anglican churches.[200] This influenced the parish's decision to build the new church in the Gothic revival style. One of the earliest Gothic churches in America, it was designed by Ithiel Town, the noted New Haven architect.

Consecrated on December 23, 1829, Christ Church has continued to serve its parish ever since. Enlarged over the years (the tower was completed in 1838), it has been the cathedral of the Episcopal Diocese of Connecticut since 1919. The cathedral is located across Main Street from the place where its predecessor of 1795 once stood. History, however, was not yet done with this earlier edifice. Having served as Hartford's first Episcopal church, it would next find new life as the city's first Catholic church.

In the early nineteenth century, Hartford was occasionally visited by Catholic priests, who would celebrate Mass for the city's then small Catholic population. On July 10, 1829, Bishop Benedict Joseph Fenwick of Boston arrived in Hartford and lodged at the City Hotel. The bishop was in town to inspect the old Episcopal church building of 1795, which the Catholics hoped to acquire for their own use. A history of the Diocese of Hartford records the following anecdote:

Opposite, top: Main Street, late 1860s. Many churches are visible in this image. *From left to right*: part of the First Baptist Church, steeple of Touro Hall (formerly the First Baptist Church), steeple of the Universalist Church of the Redeemer, steeple of St. John's Episcopal Church, steeple of Center Congregational Church (the South Baptist Church steeple can just barely be made out behind it), Melodeon Hall (formerly Fourth Congregational Church), steeple of Pearl Street Congregational Church and Christ Church. *Hartford Collection, Hartford History Center, Hartford Public Library.*

Opposite, bottom: Main Street, circa 1930. The buildings around the First Baptist Church and Christ Church Cathedral are different than in the last view. The G. Fox Building is on the left. Beyond Christ Church Cathedral are the Miller Building, Roberts Block and the store of Wise, Smith & Company. The large structure on the right is the American Industrial Building, built in 1921, and on the far right is the Leonard Building. Both were later demolished. *Hartford Collection, Hartford History Center, Hartford Public Library.*

Bishop Brownell, the Protestant Episcopal bishop, was present when Bishop Fenwick was examining the church. In the course of the conversation, Bishop Brownell remarked: "Well, Bishop Fenwick, as we have a fine new church building we will let you have the old one." Bishop Fenwick retorted, "Yes, and you have a fine new religion, and we will keep the old one."[201]

On July 14, 1829, Bishop Fenwick arranged for the purchase of the church, which was soon moved to the corner of Main and Talcott Streets. On June 17, 1830, the bishop dedicated the building as the "Church of the Holy and Undivided Trinity."[202] During the next two decades, the Catholic population in Hartford, including large numbers of Irish immigrants, increased rapidly. A larger church was badly needed. St. Patrick's Church, at the corner of Church and Ann Streets, was dedicated in 1851. With the construction of St. Patrick's, as the history of the Diocese explains,

the Church of the Holy Trinity, our first cathedral, was little used thereafter, save for an occasional marriage and baptism. On May 12, 1853, the historic old structure was destroyed by fire. As the conflagration occurred during the period when the [anti-Catholic and anti-immigrant] *Know-Nothing element was dominant in the State, it was attributed to an incendiary.[203]*

Holy Trinity Church was not rebuilt, but other Catholic churches soon followed. St. Peter's Parish, covering the southern section of the city, was established in 1859. Its original church, converted from an old school building, was replaced by the current church on Main Street in 1868. Today, St. Peter's is the oldest surviving Catholic church building in Hartford. The original St. Patrick's Church of 1851 was destroyed by a fire in 1874. The current church replaced it on the same spot in 1876. Today it is known as St. Patrick's and St. Anthony's Church, the two parishes having merged in 1958. Today, there are fourteen Catholic parishes in Hartford.

ST. JOHN'S EPISCOPAL CHURCH

While Christ Church Cathedral survives as the third oldest church on Main Street, there was once another Episcopal church located just a few blocks south. Established due to the continued overcrowding at Christ Church, St. John's Episcopal Church was built on a lot not far from the Wadsworth

Atheneum. Consecrated on April 30, 1842, it was the first church to be built to the plans of Henry Austin, a prominent New Haven architect who had an office in Hartford at the time.[204] Austin designed many buildings in the picturesque styles popular in the mid-nineteenth century. On April 25, 1842, the *Hartford Courant* reprinted a description of St. John's Church from *Chronicle of the Church*, which described the building as "a chaste and beautiful structure, in the early pointed Gothic style, built of the Chatham [Portland] free stone, with a tower projecting the full size, surmounted by a second octangular tower, the whole finished by a very graceful spire." Unlike the lower stone portion of the church, the second tower and spire were constructed of wood. Due to later structural decay, the spire was removed in 1875. The article continues:

> *The main and second towers are supported by buttresses of appropriate dimensions, surmounted by pinnacles, which are intersected by battlements. In the rear is a projection of large dimensions, in which is set a lofty window, divided by mullions. The building is lighted by eight windows, four on either side, in the same style. The ceiling is finished with an arch which spans the whole building, composed of a series of richly moulded groins, the trusses of which are sustained by highly ornamented corbels... There are side galleries, with a convenient choir over the vestibule, in which is placed an organ of superior finish, tone, and compass, with a Gothic exterior.*[205]

Various improvements were made to the church in the coming years. These included the raising of the bell in 1847, the erection of a Gothic iron fence along Main Street in 1850 and the decision, made in 1856, to excavate a basement for a furnace.[206] Further significant alterations were made around the time of the church's fiftieth anniversary. On September 8, 1891, the *Courant* noted that

> *the interior appearance of St. John's Church will be materially changed and improved by the alterations made this summer, now nearly completed. The old tower room and the organ loft choir alley, which was vacated, last year, when the organ was removed to the body of the church, have been converted into a parish room... The south staircase to the old organ gallery has been closed, and a comfortable pastor's study gained... The plans were from Cook, Hapgood & Company, who also have the contract.*[207]

Soon after the start of the new century, St. John's was preparing, like a number of other churches, to move away from downtown Hartford. The great financier J.P. Morgan wanted to donate, in memory of his father, a new art gallery building to the Wadsworth Atheneum. It was to be built on land partly occupied by St. John's Church. In 1905, the parish decided to sell its land on Main Street to the trustees of the Wadsworth Atheneum. Having declined an offer by the Atheneum five years previously, the parish was now ready to accept a raised offer of $70,000, which was considered to be "a record price for property in that vicinity." In the years since the Civil War, the nature of the neighborhood had changed from residential to commercial, and "it had long been felt that the church was not in a good location for its most efficient work."[208] Because a number of other Episcopal parishes had been established in nearby parts of Hartford, St. John's Parish decided to rebuild in an area then being developed, just across the city line in West Hartford. The new church, designed by Bertram G. Goodhue, was constructed on Farmington Avenue in 1907–09.[209]

On July 11, 1907, a *Courant* story entitled "Preparing for New Atheneum Addition" observed that the ruins of the church were like "the defunct carcass of a whale on the seashore...Its roof beams dispelled of their covering of slate stood out against the sky like so many ribs." The story continues:

> *Sometimes there have been whole walls, twenty feet high or so, around which ropes have been slung, at which the whole available force of Italian [workers] and of small boys inevitably present at such an occasion, have tugged in unison, keeping time to the monotonous "Heave, heave" of the boss, until they fell amid a blinding and chocking cloud of dust and the approving cries of some of the more youthful spectators.*

Whenever an old church was demolished, there was great interest in the contents of the cornerstone. In a ceremony on July 14, 1841, Bishop Brownell had laid the cornerstone of St. John's Church and an address was delivered by Reverend Abner Jackson, professor of ancient languages at Washington (Trinity) College.[210] Sixty-six years later, on July 27, 1907, the *Courant* reported that

> *there was a little touch of old Hartford yesterday morning at the ruins of old St. John's Church on Main Street...when the corner stone of the church was removed. Some interest had, of course, been felt as to what would be found under the corner stone. Added to this was the fear that some marauders might pry off the stone some night when no one was around,*

to see if they could get something valuable from under it. Because of the removal of most of the stone work above the corner stone this would have been a comparatively easy task. Accordingly it was decided to take out the corner-stone and the officers of the church were on hand.

Inside was found a copper box. On top of it was discovered a half-dollar from 1840, on which had been stamped the name James Ward. It was concluded that the coin had probably been thrown onto the box at the last moment before it was sealed in the cornerstone. The recovered box was not opened until September, when the *Courant* reported that there was "bitter disappointment," because "in place of the Bible, prayer-book and other papers sealed in it, nothing but an unrecognizable mass of mould was found."[211]

HARTFORD'S FIRST BAPTIST CHURCH

Before members of his denomination began holding regular Sunday meetings in Hartford in 1789, Deacon John Bolles and other Baptists would make a weekly trek north to attend services at the Baptist church in Suffield. Under Bolles's leadership, a church in Hartford was officially constituted on March 23, 1790. At first, their meetings took place in private homes. In 1798, they built a church at the southeast corner of Market and Temple Streets.[212] A gable-front building, the church lacked a steeple at first, although a notice, appearing in the *Courant* of March 19, 1798, stated that

proposals will be received from any person willing to contract for erecting a Tower and Spire, for the Baptist Meeting-House in this City—the dimentions [sic] *of which must be as follows, viz. The Tower to be 14 feet square, and in height and diameter in proportion to the Tower. The whole to be done in a plain, but workmanlike manner. The proposals must include all the materials, together with the erecting and finishing the same complete. The payment to be made in a valuable tract of New Land, on the banks of Connecticut river. Proposals will likewise be received for finishing the inside of said house. Payment as above.*

It was not until the pastorate of Reverend Elisha Cushman (1812–25), that the building "was raised, a basement was provided, a tower or cupola added, and a church bell placed in the tower."[213] In 1823, the first classes of

Old Baptist Church, Market Street. *From a postcard, courtesy of Tomas Nenortas.*

Washington (now Trinity) College met in the building.[214] The Baptists used this church on Market Street until they moved to Main Street in 1831. The old church continued to serve a variety of functions, until it was finally slated for demolition in 1911 to make way for a new fire station. It continued for a time as a house of worship for other denominations. From 1842 to 1854, it was home to an Adventist congregation and then became the second home of the Warburton Chapel Sunday school, during which time it was called the Market Street Chapel. It next hosted the meetings of Hartford's Washingtonian Temperance Society. Significant changes were then made when the building became the property of a German society, which used it as a gymnasium. Around this time, the tower was removed. After 1868, the former church was utilized as an office and workshop by a series of companies that produced sash windows, doors and blinds.

With its destruction imminent in 1911, a reporter described his visit to the venerable but neglected structure:

The building presents but a sorry imitation of its former self...The clap-boards are worn and rotted, their covering, of buff-colored paint as broken in texture as a peek-a-boo shirtwaist. Various attempts at improvements in years past—and the attempts have amounted to scores perhaps—show in the construction like oases in a desert. The long, narrow windows, so noticeable in types of the old "meetin'-house," are blindless and hold glass panes cracked, or broken and generally pretty nearly opaque. Out of the tower window which is semi-circular and the only touch of symmetry in the severe construction lines of the building, there hangs what was once an American flag, disheveled, its colors run and entirely in keeping, as it were, with the general appearance of the building.

Inside, where "holes made by the removal of the trapeze bars are still apparent in the ceilings," he observed that

one would hardly realize he was in what was once a church...On the upper floor there are some traces of the more spiritual days of the building. The ceiling is high—as in all old meeting houses—and square solid pillars border the auditorium and still contain some of the blue and gold paint probably bestowed upon them by the Adventists during their occupation. In the rear, a narrow gallery marks what was once a choir and organ loft. The old stairways leading to the loft, is chocked with debris, accumulated during an era or so past.[215]

BAPTIST CHURCHES ON MAIN STREET

The cornerstone of the first Baptist church to be constructed on Main Street was laid on April 30, 1830, and the house was dedicated on March 23, 1831.[216] A brick Greek revival edifice with a steeple, it served the Baptists until 1853. From 1856 to 1876, while it was home to Congregation Beth Israel, it was known as Touro Hall.[217] It was then torn down to make way for the Cheney Building, designed by H.H. Richardson, a Hartford landmark that still stands today.

Not long after it was built, the 1831 church "was soon filled to overflowing,"[218] and it was found necessary to have a second Baptist church in the city. According to a history of the First Baptist Church, the new South Baptist Church was formed October 17, 1834, and "[t]heir first house of worship on Main and Sheldon streets was erected through the joint contributions of the new and the mother church."[219] Like the First Baptist Church, the South Baptist Church was a Greek revival building and had a similar square steeple. In 1852, when a new South Baptist Church was being built, it was sold to the society of Presbyterians.[220] This congregation used it until 1868, when the current First Presbyterian Church was dedicated on College Street (now Capitol Avenue). On March 11, 1868, the *Courant* reported that

> *the old Presbyterian church, on the corner of Main and Sheldon streets, is rapidly becoming transformed into a far different structure from what it has hitherto been. The windows on the north and south side have been cut down to the basement, to give light to the two stores which are to be built underneath, fronting on Sheldon street…The upper part of the building will be fitted up into a hall…which will be used for dancing parties, concerts or lectures, and will no doubt be very popular at the south end…The present front of the building is to be taken out and a new one erected of pressed brick, on the building line, forward of its present location…The steeple was mostly taken down on Tuesday. The floorings of the steeple were cut away, and then the bell lowered and loaded upon a wagon, between 3 and 5 p.m., Monday, which was pretty lively work. At the present rate a few weeks will see the job complete, and the stores and hall ready for occupancy.[221]*

The former church, thus altered to serve commercial purposes, does not survive today.

In the 1850s, both the First and South Baptist Societies built new churches constructed of the popular Portland brownstone on Main Street. Changing architectural tastes led both churches to switch from Greek revival buildings to edifices designed in the Romanesque revival style. On November 4, 1852, the cornerstone of a new South Baptist Church was laid at a site across the street from the old church, which had just recently been sold to the Presbyterians. The church, designed by Thomas Alexander Tefft of Providence, Rhode Island, was dedicated on April 23, 1854, although the steeple was completed later.[222] Three days before the dedication, the *Courant* reported that

> *the building is one of the most imposing in the city, and reflects great credit on the skill of the artist who planned it, and the taste of the Society who followed out the plan. In the serene, solemn, heavy style of Architecture, it*

South Baptist Church, Main Street, built 1852–54. *Courtesy of Tomas Nenortas.*

has no rival in Connecticut. Every part is in good keeping with the general plan, and though every thing is grand and massive there is nothing repulsive or gloomy, especially in the interior finish. The conference or lecture room is carried out in the same style, and is one of the finest in the city... The Church is an ornament to the city, and a proof of the progress of architectural taste among us.[223]

With the erection of the new South Baptist Church, "the First Church felt that the time had come likewise for them to secure a church edifice fully up to the new requirements."[224] In 1853, the church purchased the Talcott lot, at the corner of Main and Talcott Streets (a small confectioner's shop stood there at the time).[225] The cornerstone was laid on March 28, 1855, and the church was dedicated on April 23, 1856, "three years to the day after the dedication of the South Baptist Church."[226] The architect of the church was "W. Russell West of Philadelphia, a relative, it is said, of the celebrated artist, Benjamin West." The chairman of the building committee was James G. Batterson.[227] One of Hartford's most prominent businessmen, Batterson was a supplier of stone for monuments and buildings. His New England Granite Works would produce some of the nation's most prominent Civil War monuments.[228] He would also found Travelers Insurance in 1863.

According to a description in the *Hartford Courant* of the new First Baptist Church, "The plan is cruciform, with vestibules in front and a tower at the south-west corner; yet owing to the singular shape of the lot, the tower is nearly on a line with the centre of the audience room or body of the church." A later history of the church elaborated:

The lot on which it is erected is diagonal, and both taxed the ingenuity and brought out the genius of the architect. The building is really in two parts, the front containing the tower, the vestibule, the vestry adjoining, all on the first floor, and the chapel on the second floor over the vestibule and the vestry...The crooked lot suggested to Mr. Batterson this broad entrance, and was by him suggested to the architect.[229]

Several features of the main audience room attracted the attention of the *Courant*:

Moulded ribs divide the arched ceilings into compartments, and in the centre of each severey at the intersection of the ribs is a foliaged boss, perforated for ventilation. The foul air is conveyed to an octagon turret, over the centre

First Baptist Church, Main Street, built 1855–56. *Courtesy of Tomas Nenortas.*

of the house. As the turret is in keeping with the style of the building, the unsightliness of the common ventilators is avoided. The Windows are all glazed with stained glass, deep blue and orange being the prevailing tints at the sides of the church, and ruby in the Clerestory. Color is also more freely used on the walls and ceilings, than has hitherto been the custom in this city. The somber drab which has so long been the orthodox hue of church walls, has been discarded for more positive tints. The ceilings have a pale blue ground, with buff ribs.[230]

Like the later Park Congregational Church, First Baptist lacked a spire, "the unfinished tower, resting on its literal foundation of rock, silently, patiently waiting for a summons to go up higher."[231] William F. O'Neil, who, as described above, had the contract to demolish the Pearl Street

Congregational Church in 1899 lamented to a reporter of the *Courant*: "There is the First Baptist Church without a spire. Now if someone would come along with a balloon and lift this spire from here and set it on that church tower it would be luck for me."[232]

The First Baptist Church's constrained lot precluded expansion. On the other hand, the South Baptist Church had room to grow, so in 1923, the two merged to form the Central Baptist Church. South Baptist's 1854 edifice was soon demolished to make way for a new church building, which was dedicated in 1926. While it was under construction, the united congregation worshiped in the old First Baptist Church. That building was sold to G. Fox & Company, which razed it in 1927. Hartford's 1926 Central Baptist Church proudly remains on Main Street.

METHODIST CHURCHES

Hartford's first Methodist church was built in 1821 at the northwest corner of Chapel and Trumbull Streets. A Greek revival edifice with a steeple, it was improved in 1840 to commemorate the centennial of Methodism. Twenty years later, the congregation moved west, to a new brownstone church on Asylum Street west of Ann Street. The former church building was converted to commercial use. It was used as an office and woodworking shop by local builder and architect John C. Mead from 1879 until his death in 1889. Others continued the business until the building was finally torn down in 1916.[233]

The new First Methodist Church on Asylum Street was an impressive Romanesque revival structure. On the northeast corner was a 64-foot tower, containing the church bell, while on the northwest corner was an imposing octagonal tower, 106 feet high.[234] In 1905, the church moved to its current building, located on Farmington Avenue, near the city's western edge. The Hartford Electric Light Company owned the old church building on Asylum for a time but eventually sold it to be converted into shops and a theater. The *Courant* reported on its transformation on April 15, 1911:

> *The entire front and towers have disappeared, while the present front of the building, which is now several feet further back from the sidewalk than the old front was, and which was previously a wooden partition, has been rebuilt into a solid brick wall.*

The first two church edifices of the First Methodist Church. *From a postcard, courtesy of Tomas Nenortas.*

The wall was built using bricks from the demolished front:

There are still profuse heaps of brick and mortar, tower stones and other debris lying about, but two dump carts and willing lumpers with their wheelbarrows are fast cleaning up and leveling off the ground, tearing up the old stone steps, and removing here and there the miscellaneous wreckage, which still stands as a small monument to what once was.[235]

In use for a number of years, the entire building was later demolished.

Another Methodist church was located nearby on Pearl Street. The African Methodist Episcopal Zion Church was formed in 1833 by members who split away from the African American church on Talcott Street. At first located in a building on Elm Street, after 1857, the AME Zion Church was based at the southwest corner of Pearl Street and Ann Streets. On November 13, 1898, the church laid the cornerstone for a new building at

Old AME Zion Church, Pearl Street. *Taylor Collection, State Archives, Connecticut State Library.*

that location, which was consecrated on Easter Sunday, April 15, 1900. As early as 1916, however, there were negotiations to sell the church property and move farther north in Hartford. The church was interested in moving into the 1874 North Methodist Church building and selling its old Pearl Street property to the city's fire department, which wanted to expand its headquarters building next door. The amount of $55,000 offered by the fire board was considered too low, and the church continued to hold out for several years, even when the city filed a condemnation suit to acquire the property on the principle of eminent domain. Finally, in 1922, the church agreed to sell to the city for $120,000. The church was able to remain in the Pearl Street building for three years while seeking a new home. The church was finally demolished in 1925, and the new fire department headquarters built on the site was completed the following year and still stands today.[236] Since 1926, the Metropolitan AME Zion Church has occupied the former North Methodist Church building at 2051 Main Street.

UNITARIAN AND UNIVERSALIST CHURCHES

In the nineteenth century, both a Unitarian and a Universalist church were established in Downtown Hartford. These two institutions continue in existence today, although one is now located on the western edge of the city and the other is in the neighboring town of West Hartford. The two denominations consolidated on the national level in 1961, forming the Unitarian Universalist Association.

The First Independent Universalist Church in the city of Hartford was built in 1824 on Central Row, facing the Old State House. A Federal-style edifice, it went through a number of alterations over the years. In 1833, the floor was raised and the front rebuilt to include space that could be rented to businesses (early tenants included a barber shop, a bathing establishment and a grocery store).[237] The interior was altered in 1852, as described by the *Hartford Times* (and quoted in the *Hartford Courant*):

> *The arched ceilings and the walls have been painted in fresco; back of the pulpit is an imitation alcove or recess, which adds greatly to the general appearance. On each side of this alcove are painted Corinthian columns. The galleries have been altered so as to run on a straight line, instead of the amphitheatre style, as before, which rendered the interior of this church so different from any other in this city.[238]*

In 1860, the Universalists moved to a new church on Main Street, across from Center Church and the Ancient Burying Ground, which is the city's oldest cemetery, dating back to the colonial era. Called the Church of the Redeemer, it was designed by Edward Behl. According to a description in the *Courant* on November 1, 1860:

> *The church edifice is one of the most beautiful in the State. The designs are chaste and elegant from their simplicity…The tower on the southwest corner is 110 feet high, and in this the bell is suspended. The material of which the whole is constructed is brick with brown stone trimmings.*

Later improvements were also made to the interior of this church. On November 14, 1889, the *Courant* praised its new paint colors, noting that the "effect is happily rather dark, and it is thus entirely free from the glaring lights which try the eyes so much in some edifices."[239] As before, the church made use of rental property to raise income. In 1899, a substantial

Universalist Church of the
Redeemer, Main Street, built
1860. *Courtesy of Tomas Nenortas.*

commercial block was erected on the lawn directly in front of the church.
The first floor contained retail shops, the second floor offices and the third
and fourth floors were apartments. The church could be reached through a
vestibule in the center of the first floor of the new building. The entrances to
the stores were on either side of this broad open corridor, which ended in a
marble stairway leading to the vestibule of the church. It was an impressive
building in the Renaissance revival style:

> *The first story is to be of white marble and the upper stories of light
> Pompeiian pressed brick with ornate terra-cotta trimmings. The efforts of
> the committee entrusted with this project, assisted by the architects, Bayley
> & Goodrich, have been directed toward securing a building which shall, at
> the same time yield the society a handsome income, and a credible addition
> to the list of noteworthy public buildings of the city.*[240]

In the end, this building would exist only until 1906. The church sold its property to Travelers, which demolished the existing structures and began to build its new headquarters on the site. The next Universalist church was built on Asylum Avenue, near where it intersects today with Cogswell Street. This church also does not survive because in 1931, the Universalists moved west again, this time to their fourth and current church, located on Fern Street in West Hartford.

Hartford's First Unitarian Society was formed in 1844. The Unitarian Church of the Saviour, designed by Minard Lafever, was dedicated on April 22, 1846. It stood at the northeast corner of Trumbull and Asylum Streets. Debts arising from the church's extravagant price tag were a severe burden on the society, which was forced to suspend services in 1857. The society soon sold its Trumbull Street property to the Charter Oak Bank,[211] and the church building itself was then moved westward to become Trinity Episcopal Church in the Asylum Hill neighborhood (it was used by that church until 1892).

In spite of this setback, the Unitarian church organization continued to exist, but it did not hold regular services again until 1877. Good investments eventually allowed the society to erect a new church on Pratt Street, which was dedicated on April 3, 1881. Unity Church, better known as Unity Hall, was a plain red brick structure in the Romanesque revival style, designed by John C. Mead (the same architect whose office was in the former First Methodist Church on Chapel Street).[212] The building was intended to function as both a church and a public hall. The *Courant* described it:

> *The arrangement of the interior is a novel departure from the traditional church auditorium, but it will be found both convenient and comfortable. If it were not for the magnificent organ at the rear of the platform, one would suppose himself to be in a miniature opera house. The seats are regular opera chairs, and are arranged in horse-shoe form. There is a gallery, and the platform is arranged like a stage, with retiring rooms on each side. The desk is to be movable, and the stage can be used for concerts, light theatricals, etc. In fact, the auditorium is just adapted to entertainments where an audience of not more than 500 or 600 is expected.*[213]

In 1914, the interior was renovated and repainted, with results that astounded one observer, who described the change as "almost a piece of magic." This writer for the *Courant* explained that the auditorium *ha*[d] *been transformed by the substitution for the former color scheme, an effect so rich and elegant, yet withal so restful, that at the time of first entry one is with difficulty persuaded that he has not hopelessly lost his way... When one steps into the auditorium, the pleasing green of the seats, the splendid oak of the chancel, the exquisite light of the walls and ceiling and the appropriate plain color green of the soft, thick carpeting create at once a composite effect that nearly baffles description.*[211]

Unity Hall was later demolished, and the Unitarian Society has since occupied two other buildings in Hartford. It first moved to a new church on Pearl Street, designed by Milton E. Hayman. This building was later sold to Ados Israel, an Orthodox Jewish congregation, which remained there until the mid-1980s. The Unitarians' current meetinghouse, designed by Victor Lundy, was built in 1961–64 on Bloomfied Avenue. Both of these later buildings survive today.

REMEMBERING HARTFORD'S VANISHED CHURCHES

The history of Hartford's lost church buildings comprises numerous houses of worship built in different sizes and architectural styles. Many later merged with other churches and moved away from the center of the city, but in the nineteenth century, their various towers and steeples were among the city's most notable landmarks. The middle years of that century saw the establishment of a significant number of new churches. In 1852, when thirty-five members of Center Church were dismissed to join others in forming the new Pearl Street Congregational Church, the usual Thursday evening lecture "was given up to a meeting for reminiscences and farewells." A Deacon Turner recalled that "our pastor is the only one who remains of those who were in the city when I came here." At that time, about thirty years before, there had been only four places of worship: Center Church, South Church, the original Christ Church and the old Baptist Church on Market Street. Center Church's pastor, Dr. Joel Hawes, responded with much emotion:

Each successive withdrawal of this kind makes a deeper impression upon me. Jacob in his old age was more affected by parting from Benjamin, than from Joseph and Simeon before. Four times I have witnessed a scene like this. In 1824 ninety-seven members left us to the North or Third Church; in 1832 eighteen to the Fourth Church, and in 1851 eight to the Presbyterian Church. But this enterprise has ever had my cordial good wishes, and if I have access to the throne of grace, I shall remember it there.[245]

NOTES

CHAPTER ONE

1. Rathbun, "Backward Glances," no. 1, 42.
2. *Hartford Courant*, "Alarm of Fire," November 14, 1850.
3. Ibid., "Central Row to be Torn Down," September 25, 1855.
4. Andrews and Ransom, *Structures and Styles*, 14.
5. *Hartford Courant*, "Travelers Buys Marble Building," February 1, 1925.
6. Close, *History of Hartford Streets*, 79.
7. Trumbull, *Memorial History*, vol. 1, 469; *Hartford Courant*, "The City Hotel Property," July 27, 1869.
8. *Hartford Courant*, "Building Permits for the Week," December 14, 1912; "Robbins Block to be Remodeled," May 7, 1914; "New Theater Opens Tomorrow," May 24, 1914.
9. Ibid., "D'Esopo Building Ready to Open," June 1, 1916.
10. Herbert J. Stoeckel, "Hartford...Then and Now," *Hartford Courant*, March 31, 1957.
11. *Hartford Courant*, "Café Under the Skies," June 7, 1900.
12. Rathbun, "Backward Glances," no. 2, 104.
13. *Hartford Courant*, "U.S. Hotel Hartford," May 26, 1829; "Rockwood's United States Hotel," August 22, 1855; "Improvements in Our Streets," May 3, 1859; "Old 'States' Hotel Prominent at One Time in City's Life," April 15, 1923.
14. Ibid., "Eagle Hotel," October 25, 1851; April 13, 1855; "Colonel Rood to Retire," February 29, 1888; "An Old Hostelry Gone," March 25, 1897.

15. Ibid., "The 'United States,'" May 5, 1869.

16. Ibid., "No Longer a Hotel," November 13, 1899.

17. Woodward, *One Hundred Years*, 98.

18. *Hartford Courant*, "Hartford National Bank in Its Handsome New Home," September 20, 1912.

19. Ibid., "Plans for a New Vaudeville House. To Replace Hartford National Bank Building," July 20, 1912.

20. Ibid., "The Exchange Bank—Handsome Front," September 3, 1869; "Exchange Bank to Become Restaurant," March 21, 1917.

21. Ibid., "Boston Caledonian Games," August 17, 1894; "The Gregory Building," March 5, 1909; "Many Sportsmen Frequented Long's," October 2, 1921; Herbert J. Stoeckel, "It's a Long Story..." *Hartford Courant*, October 21, 1962.

22. *Hartford Courant*, "American Hotel to Be Torn Down," March 30, 1925; Herbert J. Stoeckel, "Hartford...Then and Now," *Hartford Courant*, May 26, 195, and September 13, 1959.

23. *Hartford in 1912*, 223–24.

24. *Hartford Courant*, "The Phoenix Bank," May 16, 1873.

25. Burpee, *First Century of the Phoenix National Bank*, 94–95.

26. *Hartford Courant*, April 23, 1850.

27. Ibid., "State Bank to Remodel Building," January 14, 1905.

28. Ibid., "Alterations in Phoenix Building," August 2, 1905.

29. Burpee, *First Century of the Phoenix National Bank*, 93.

30. *Hartford Courant*, "Phoenix Bank Lions for City Building," July 16, 1912.

31. Longstreth, *Buildings of Main Street*, 109.

32. *Hartford Courant*, "State Bank Has Fine Building," August 27, 1908.

33. Ibid., "Phoenix National Bank Will Open Its New Home Tomorrow," June 8, 1924; "Nine-Story Structure Is Beautiful Building of Dignified Design"; "17,934 at Opening of Phoenix Bank," June 10, 1924.

CHAPTER TWO

34. *Evolution of a Building Lot*, 30–31.

35. *Hartford Courant*, "The Travelers Insurance Company," November 1, 1872.

36. As the first commissioner of the U.S. Patent Office in Washington, Henry Ellsworth became a champion of the telegraph, which had recently been invented by Samuel F.B. Morse. Ellsworth's daughter, Annie (who had been born in the Ellsworth House), suggested the world's first telegraph

message, sent on May 24, 1844, from Washington to Baltimore, to Morse: "What hath God wrought."

37. *Evolution of a Building Lot*, 39; *Hartford Courant*, "Travelers Buys All Three Blocks," January 4, 1905.

38. *Evolution of a Building Lot*, 39.

39. Ibid., 28–29.

40. *Hartford Courant*, "Building Improvements," December 14, 1865; "The Aetna in Its Handsome New Home," June 8, 1905.

41. Ibid., "Aetna's Woodwork Destroyed by Fire," January 7, 1905.

42. Ibid., "The Old Courant Office and the First Bible," April 28, 1869.

43. Ibid., "The Toucey Place." November 12, 1868.

44. Ibid., "Charter Oak Life Building," November 18, 1868.

45. Ibid., "Removing Staging at Aetna Building." October 29, 1914.

CHAPTER THREE

46. Love, *Colonial History of Hartford*, 158.

47. *Hartford Courant*, "Pearl Street—One of Hartford's Busiest Streets," August 21, 1921.

48. Burpee, *One Hundred Years of Service*, 41–42; Love, *Colonial History of Hartford*, 316; Leverett Belknap, "History of Main Street from Pearl to Asylum," *Hartford Courant*, June 8, 1924; Herbet J. Stoeckel, "Hartford… Then and Now," *Hartford Courant*, June 9, 1957; *Hartford Courant*, "City Improvements—Union Hall," May 10, 1871.

49. *Hartford Courant*, "The Connecticut Mutual Building. History of the Enterprise—Full Description of the Structure, etc," September 3, 1869.

50. Ibid., "Connecticut Mutual. Description of the Proposed New Structure," April 7, 1900.

51. Ibid., "Connecticut Mutual to Build. Interesting Discovery Yesterday on the Church Site," June 1, 1900.

52. Ibid., "Excavating on Pearl Street," July 21, 1900.

53. Ibid., "Connecticut Mutual. Description of the Proposed New Structure," April 7, 1900.

54. Ibid., "In New Quarters," April 12, 1902.

55. Ibid., "Connecticut Mutual. Public Improves Opportunity to Inspect Its Handsome Building," May 4, 1903.

56. Ibid., "Connecticut Mutual. Description of the Proposed New Structure," April 7, 1900.

57. Ibid., "New Building for Bank Is Progressing," July 1, 1928; ibid., "Hartford's Oldest Bank Occupies New Quarters," December 16, 1928.

58. Ibid., "'Old Bank' Plans to Move into Tower Building in April; Tenants Come Later," February 20, 1966.

59. Forrest Morgan, "Life and Accident Insurance," in Trumbull, *Memorial History*, vol. 1, 513.

60. Ralph W. Chapin, "Old State Bank Building Housed Slave Insurers," *Hartford Courant*, January 19, 1928.

61. *Hartford Courant*, "It Is Squad A Now," June 10, 1910; "Squad A Departs from Pearl Street," June 22, 1921; "Old Fire Bell May Come Back," August 22, 1921; "History of the City of Hartford Fire Department," http://fire.hartford.gov/history/history.htm.

62. *Hartford Courant*, "State Savings Bank to Build on Pearl Street," July 21, 1921; "State Savings Bank In New Pearl Street Home," October 29, 1922; "Remodeling Work Shown Public by State Savings Bank," November 7, 1950.

63. Ibid., "The National Fire. Its Elegant New Home on Pearl Street," September 1, 1893.

64. *Hartford, Conn.*, 56.

65. *Hartford Courant*, "Phoenix Life Building," March 28, 1896; "Phoenix's New Home," September 18, 1896.

66. Ibid., "Phoenix Mutual Life. Its Elegant Suite of Offices in its New Building," June 19, 1897.

67. Ibid., "Enlargement Plans of Phoenix Mutual Life Insurance Company," October 18, 1915.

68. Ibid., "Pearl St. Property Sold for $800,000," October 7, 1924; "Standard Fire Moves to Phoenix Mutual Building," June 21, 1926.

69. Ibid., "Erection of New Judd & Company Building to Cost $500,000," September 9, 1923; "Judd & Company Occupy New Building Oct. 1," March 23, 1924; "Fine Building in Financial District," November 16, 1924; "Dime Savings Bank to Have New Home," December 12, 1924; "Dime Savings Bank Is to Occupy New Home Tomorrow," November 22, 1925.

70. Maryellen Fillo, "A Building's Name Holds History. Florence Gates Judd Was in the Upper Crust," *Hartford Courant*, September 29, 2002.

71. David S. Barrett, "Blast Crumbles 9-Story Building in 10 Seconds," *Hartford Courant*, July 30, 1973.

72. *Hartford Courant*, "Phoenix Fire's Building is Sold," January 25, 1905; "New Building on Pearl Street. The Connecticut General Life to Erect It," May 3, 1906; "New Buildings and Other Improvements," Febraury 18,

1907; "Permit for New Home for Conn. General Company," September 5, 1919; "Insurance Firm to Use Old Offices," July 3, 1949; "Mechanics Bank Buys Property. To Enlarge Quarters in Old Conn. General Building, Pearl Street," September 21, 1950.

73. Ibid., "$125,000 Realty Deal on Pearl Street," March 15, 1917; "Bank Building Has Strength, Dignity," February 22, 1925; *Hartford Times*, "Mechanics Bank Opens New Quarters," February 13, 1953; *Hartford Courant*, "Mechanics Savings to Spend $1 Million for Renovation," September 10, 1972.

74. *Hartford Courant*, "New Bank Building Nearing Completion," October 17, 1919; "Mutual Bldg. Sold to Riverside," April 4, 1925; "Richter Company Opens Home Tomorrow," May 16, 1926; "Local Bank Will Expand Plant Space," May 21, 1937; "Charter Oak Bank Buys United Bank Building," December 17, 1968.

75. Ibid., "Office Building to be Erected on Pearl Street," August 5, 1934.

76. Ibid., "Silas Chapman, Jr. Leaves Old Stand. Insurance Man Leases Corning Residence," May 30, 1914.

77. Love, *Colonial History of Hartford*, 228.

78. Caroline M. Hewins, "The Public Buildings of Hartford," in Twitchell, *Hartford in History*, 160.

79. Herber J. Stoeckel, "Hartford ... Then and Now," *Hartford Courant*, July 27, 1958.

80. *Hartford Courant*, "The Hartford Fire Insurance Company's Building," August 18, 1869.

81. Ibid., "Hartford Fire, 'Old Original,'" October 6, 1908; "Hartford Fire's Building," July 12, 1899.

82. Ibid., "Explosion of Gas," October 31, 1893; "O'Gorman's Fatal Fall," April 13, 1897.

83. Love, *Colonial History of Hartford*, 289–92.

84. *Hartford, Conn.*, 96–97.

85. *Hartford Courant*, "Pearl Street Improvements," July 1, 1865; "A Fearful Crash! The City Bindery in Ruins!" May 2, 1866; "The Falling of the City Bindery Building—Large Loss of Property," May 3, 1866; "To Tear Down Old Case, Lockwood & Brainard Building," December 28, 1927; "Print Plant Marks 100th Anniversary," January 9, 1936.

86. Ibid., "Plimpton Store Now Remodeled and Restocked," May 25, 1922; "Telephone Company's Fine New Home," March 2, 1911; "Telephone Home Near Completion," August 16, 1920; "Excellent Example of 'Open Shop' Building Construction in Hartford," November 5, 1923; "New Telephone Building Erected to Meet City's Growing Service Needs," August 30, 1931.

87. Ibid., "New 'Y' Building to be Open for Use February 27," February 19, 1939; "YMCA to Remodel, Expand," May 22, 1968; "Concerned Organization Trying to Save YMCA," November 1, 1973; Bruce Kauffman, "YMCA Leaders Seek Study on City Building," *Hartford Courant*, February 14, 1974; "YMCA to Raze Old Building," February 20, 1974; *Hartford Courant*, "Vigil Continues at YMCA Site," March 3, 1974; David S. Barrett, "City Halts Razing of Y Building," *Hartford Courant*, March 6, 1974; *Hartford Courant*, "Insurance Is Approved for YMCA Demolition," March 6, 1974.

CHAPTER FOUR

88. Trumbull, *Memorial History*, vol. 1, 662.

89. *Hartford Courant*, "Next Year's Paving," December 31, 1896.

90. Ibid., "Widening Asylum Street," January 6, 1897; "Asylum Street Corner," January 14, 1897; "To Have a Round Corner," January 18, 1897.

91. Ibid., "Isle of Safety on State Street," July 25, 1912; "To Build Isle of Safety at City Hall," February 13, 1913; "That Isle of Safety," February 24, 1914.

92. Ibid., "The Catlin Building," August 30, 1900.

93. Ibid., "Old Hartford Bank to Change Location," July 3, 1907.

94. Ibid., "Bank Bldg. to be Made into Stores," September 8, 1928.

95. Ibid., "The Trumbull House," March 9, 1853.

96. Ibid., "The Great Hotel on Asylum Street," May 1, 1856.

97. Ibid., November 13, 1857.

98. Herbert J. Stoeckel, "Hartford Then…and Now," *Hartford Courant*, July 17, 1960.

99. J.G. Rathbun, "The Old Allyn House," *Hartford Courant*, October 13, 1899.

100. *Hartford Courant*, "New Allyn House," July 16, 1898; "The New Allyn House," October 13, 1899.

101. Ibid., "Old Memories Will Be Orphans When the Allyn House Dies," June 26, 1960.

102. Ibid., "Asylum Street—A New Hall at Last," January 31, 1860; "Sale of Allyn Hall," December 11, 1894; "Auditorium Sold to W.W. Walker Company," February 25, 1905; "Was Allyn Hall in Days of Yore," February 27, 1914.

103. Ibid., "Majestic Theater's Sign Blazes Forth," January 8, 1915.

104. Ibid., "Asylum Street—A New Hall at Last," January 31, 1860

105. Ibid., December 13, 1856; J.G. Rathbun, "The Old Allyn House,"

Hartford Courant, October 13, 1899; "The New Goodwin Block," July 25, 1890.

106. Ibid., "Plaut Company to Open 20th Store Here," December 5, 1923; "Garber Bros. Take Asylum Street Store," February 5, 1933; "Garber Bros.; Buy Old Morgan House," Februaruy 6, 1926; "Modern Bldg. to Replace Morgan Home," April 24, 1927; "Slalz Leases Morgan Bldg. Store Space," August 29, 1928; "Building Is Acquired by Flint-Bruce," March 29, 1942; "Resolute Group Is Moving into Morgan Office," November 11, 1960.

107. Close, *History of Hartford Streets*, 4; *Hartford Courant*, "Boardman's New Building," April 2, 1878; "J.M. Ney Company Moves into New Quarters," June 26, 1917; "D'Esopo Tenants," August 5, 1921; "Asylum Street Block Sold for $200,000," May 14, 1925.

108. Ibid., "Handsome New Building," June 24, 1895; "Hartford Life Insurance Company," October 6, 1908; Mike Swift and Linda Giuca, "Frank's to Close, and with It an Era," *Hartford Courant*, April 4, 1995.

109. Steiner, *History of Education*, 52.

110. Barnard, *School Architecture*, 214–15.

111. *Hartford Courant*, "Real Estate Sales," February 25, 1870; "Asylum Street Improvements," March 16, 1871; "The Foster Block Sold," August 7, 1905; Kevin Thomas, "Archdiocese to Raze Weldon Building; Development Plans for Site Not Certain," *Hartford Courant*, March 31, 1982; Donaghue, *Two Boxes*, 2–7.

112. *Hartford Courant*, "Important Sale of Real Estate," October 1, 1866.

113. Ibid., "Proprietor of Garde Hotel Dead," January 29, 1907; "Management of Hotel Garde to Change," August 2, 1913; "Hotel Garde Goes to Fred H. Meyer," May 23, 1916; "Hotel Garde Company Bankrupt Court Is Told," October 12, 1918.

114. Ibid., "Will Not Change Hotel Garde Lobby," February 15, 1920.

115. William Cockerham, "Hotel Garde Proposed as Housing for Elderly," *Hartford Courant*, February 6, 1970; Laurence Cohen, "Grand Era Ends for Garde Hotel," *Hartford Courant*, November 1, 1973; *Hartford Courant*, "Group Aims to Keep Garde Hotel Alive," November 2, 1973.

CHAPTER FIVE

116. *Remembering G. Fox* (Connecticut Historical Society).

117. *Hartford Courant*, "G. Fox's New Store," January 19, 1881.

118. Ibid., "Fatal Fire Yesterday," January 10, 1887.

119. *Hartford Weekly Times*, "A $120,000 Blaze. Burning of the Averill Block. Three Merchants Burned Out. Death of a Brave Man," January 13, 1887.

120. *Hartford Courant*, "The Averill Building," April 8, 1887.

121. Ibid., "G. Fox & Company's Big Department Store and Woolworth's 5 and 10 Cent Store Destroyed in Billows of Flame," January 30, 1917.

122. Ibid., "Tense Emotion Through Crowd," January 30, 1917

123. Ibid., "Out to See the Ruins," January 31, 1917; "When Will Fox's Fire Burn Out?" February 3, 1917; "Watchman Blamed for $750,000 Fire," February 13, 1917.

124. Ibid., "Important Business Changes," February 10, 1881; "G.M. Talcott Assigns. Sale of His Main and Pratt Street Block," February 8, 1889; "Sage, Allen & Company's Opening," April 17, 1889.

125. Ibid., "Valuable Real Estate Sold," August 23, 1895; "Business Change. Firm of Sage, Allen & Company is Dissolved," December 25, 1903; "Romance of Building Up Public Serving Business Organization: Story of Sage-Allen & Company," June 10, 1923; "Market St. Site First Step in New Sage-Allen Growth," April 10, 1955.

126. Ibid., "New Main Street Block," March 31, 1904; "Sage, Allen to Enlarge," April 6, 1904; "Greatly Enlarged Stores," March 13, 1911; "Innovations at Sage, Allen & Company Store," February 27, 1916; "Sage-Allen Company Gives Reception," March 22, 1917; "Romance of Building Up Public Serving Business Organization: Story of Sage-Allen & Company," June 10, 1923.

127. Herbert J. Stockel, "Hartford Then…and Now," *Hartford Courant*, September 7, 1958.

128. William C. Brocklesby, "Architecture in Hartford," in Trumbull, *Memorial History*, vol. 1, 469.

129. *Hartford Courant*, "Start Excavation For Sage-Allen Addition," July 21, 1928; Wendell A. Teague, "Sage-Allen Addition Is Progressing," *Hartford Courant*, November 11, 1928; *Hartford Courant*, "Sage-Allen's New Addition Thrown Open," September 4, 1929.

130. *Hartford Courant*, "Sage-Allen to Use All of Building," September 11, 1946; *Hartford Courant*, "Sage-Allen Will Install Escalators," April 6, 1947; "Sage-Allen Store Opens New Addition," December 4, 1951; "Market St. Site First Step in New Sage-Allen Growth," April 10, 1955.

131. Ibid., "Ballerstein's Building," July 15, 1893.

132. Ibid., "Ballerstein Block Has Been Sold," February 1, 1910; "Worth, Inc. Leases Dillon Building," August 1, 1923; "For Lerner Shops. Dillon Building to be Razed," March 18, 1964.

133. Ibid., "Sage-Allen to Show New Look, Plans Expensive Face-Lifting," December 30, 1966.

134. Thomas S. Weaver, 142; *Hartford Courant*, "Wise, Smith & Company," January 14, 1897.

135. *Hartford Courant*, "Wise, Smith & Company's Opening," November 2, 1897; "Isidore Wise Tells of Store's Growth," October 11, 1917.

136. Ibid., "Robert's New Opera House," April 30, 1868; "Robert's Opera House—The Roof All On," September 10, 1868.

137. Ibid., "Wise, Smith & Company Enlargement of Business Property on Main Street," August 21, 1901; "A Growing Store," August 28, 1902; "Little Left of Wise-Smith Annex," October 21, 1905; "Roberts Property Sold to Wise, Smith & Company," July 1, 1907; "Wise, Smith & Company Continue to Grow," September 30, 1910; "Main Street Loses Historic Landmark," July 24, 1917.

138. Ibid., "Wise, Smith & Company Get Corning Property," April 16, 1910.

139. Ibid., "Wise, Smith & Company's Store a Large Modern Plant," November 22, 1911.

140. Ibid., "Wise, Smith & Company's Enlarged Store," October 12, 1912.

141. Ibid., "Wise, Smith & Company to Have New Buildings," August 5, 1916; "Hamersley Building on Pratt Street Bought by I. Wise. Will Erect Eight Story Building," June 3, 1917; "Wise Building on Pratt Street," November 21, 1917; "Wise, Smith & Company to Build Addition," June 8, 1921; "Wise, Smith & Company Buy Sage Property," July 9, 1924.

142. Ibid., "Wise, Smith New Home Is Finished," April 20, 1930; "Wise-Smith Expected to Close Doors May 8," April 21, 1954; "Korvette Spared No Costs," December 5, 1957.

143. Ibid., "Former Hartford Cash Boy's Vision Proved Wise-Smith's History," October 14, 1928.

CHAPTER SIX

144. Barber, *Connecticut Historical Collections*, 42–43.

145. Isham and Brown, *Early Connecticut Houses*, 41–43; Love, *Colonial History of Hartford*, 331.

146. Isham and Brown, *Early Connecticut Houses*, 76; Love, *Colonial History of Hartford*, 332–37.

147. Love, *Colonial History of Hartford*, 340–42; William C. Brocklesby, "Architecture in Hartford," in Trumbull, *Memorial History*, vol. 1, 466; *Hartford Courant*, "Deane House Razing Hit in Article," August 25, 1926.

148. Derby, "Riverside Cemetery," 385; Trumbull, *Memorial History*, vol. 1, 84.

149. Close, *History of Hartford Streets*, 107; *Hartford Courant*, "Building is Unsafe," September 28, 1899; "Old House to Go," July 14, 1900; Campbell, "Governor Talcott's Mansion," 359–61.

150. The two men met again in May the following year at the Webb House in Wethersfield. There they made the initial plans for the military campaign that would end in victory at the Battle of Yorktown that October.

151. http://govtrumbullhousedar.org.

152. Sigourney, *Letters of Life*, 83–91.

153. Dunham, *Reminiscences*, 30.

154. *Hartford Courant*, "Remodelling the Old Wadsworth Residence," May 19, 1881; "Start Razing of Atheneum Annex Today," July 22, 1932; Herbert J. Stoeckel, "Hartford … Then and Now." *Hartford Courant*, October 13, 1957.

155. *Hartford Courant*, "Council Votes To Restore Historic Wadsworth Barn," September 23, 1952; "$2,500 Starts Wadsworth Stable Fund. Friends of Hartford and Miss Day Move to Restore Structure," February 12, 1953; "DAR Presented Historic Stable At Ceremonies," June 6, 1954.

CHAPTER SEVEN

156. Love, *Colonial History of Hartford*, 197, 200–3; Walker, *History of the First Church*, 88–90.

157. Love, *Colonial History of Hartford*, 204, 207–8, 210.

158. Walker, *History of the First Church*, 288–89.

159. Love, *Colonial History of Hartford*, 211–12; Parker, *History of the Second Church*, 120–21, 200.

160. Parker, *History of the Second Church*, 121.

161. Weld, *History of Immanuel Church*, 5.

162. Ibid., 7–8.

163. *Hartford Courant*, "The North Church," September 3, 1866.

164. Weld, *History of Immanuel Church*, 16.

165. *Hartford Courant*, "The North Church Property," August 28, 1866; "The North Church Steeple—A Portion of It Pulled Down," September 18, 1866.

166. Ibid., "Park Congregational Church. The Plan and Appearance of the New Edifice," March 9, 1867; "Church Changes," March 17, 1921.

167. Weld, *History of Immanuel Church*, 26, 30.

168. *Hartford Courant*, "Tears Fill Eyes in Last Services in Park Church," April 20, 1914.

169. Ibid., "Fourth Church Will Move West," November 15, 1912.

170. Ibid., "The Melodeon," November 10, 1851.

171. Ibid., "The Melodeon Bell," May 24, 1855.

172. Brooks, "Fourth Congregational Church," 238.

173. *Hartford Courant*, "Dedication of the Fourth Congregational Church," April 8, 1850.

174. Brooks, "Fourth Congregational Church," 238.

175. *Hartford Courant*, "Ready to Dedicate New Fourth Church," September 12, 1914.

176. Brooks, "Fourth Congregational Church," 238.

177. Herbert J. Stoeckel, "Hartford … Then and Now," *Hartford Courant*, January 17, 1960.

178. *Hartford Courant*, "Pearl Street Church. Rev. Mr. Love Preaches a Memorial Sermon," June 26, 1899.

179. Weld, *History of Immanuel Church*, 33–40.

180. *Hartford Courant*, "Pearl Street Congregational Church," December 2, 1852.

181. Ibid., "Church Property Sold. Pearl Street Congregation Will Go West," June 26, 1897.

182. Ibid., "Pearl Street Church. Now Owned by William F. O'Neil, the Contractor," August 5, 1899.

183. Ibid., "Pearl Street Church Property," April 12, 1897.

184. Weld, *History of Immanuel Church*, 40.

185. *Hartford Courant*, "To Be Thrown Down. Pearl Street Church Spire to Fall To-day," August 16, 1899.

186. Ibid., "The Pearl Street Spire," July 17, 1899.

187. Ibid., "To Be Thrown Down. Pearl Street Church Spire to Fall To-day," August 16, 1899; "Changes His Plans," August 18, 1899.

188. Ibid., "Falling Section of the Steeple of the Pearl Street Church, Hartford," 646–47.

189. *Hartford Weekly Times*, "Waiting for Its Fall," August 26, 1899.

190. Swift, *Black Prophets*, 215; Verrett, "Faith Congregational Church," 34–35; *Hartford Courant*, "Farewell to the Talcott St. Church," March 26, 1906.

191. *Hartford Courant*, "Diamond Anniversary," November 11, 1901.

192. Ibid., "Farewell to the Talcott St. Church," March 26, 1906.

193. Ibid., "The New Talcott Street Church," April 9, 1906.

194. Michele Borders, "Church Marks 150th Year By Placing Old Cornerstone," *Hartford Courant*, June 21, 1976.

195. *Hartford Courant*, "Dedication of Warburton Chapel," June 29, 1866.

196. Ibid., "Warburton Chapel to Observe Sixty-Fiftieth Anniversary," May 28, 1916.

197. Herbert J. Stoeckel, "Hartford...Then and Now," *Hartford Courant*, June 5, 1960.

CHAPTER EIGHT

198. Lilienthal, *Christ Church Parish*, 3–7; *Contributions*, 35, 52–3.

199. *Contributions*, 56–7.

200. Lilienthal, *Christ Church Parish*, 14.

201. O'Donnell, *History of the Diocese*, 184.

202. Ibid., 185–87.

203. Ibid., 192.

204. O'Gorman, *Henry Austin*, 79–80.

205. *Hartford Courant*, "Consecration of St. John's Church, Hartford," April 25, 1842.

206. Burr, *History of St. John's Church*, 30–31.

207. *Hartford Courant*, "Changes in Churches," September 8, 1891

208. Ibid., "Atheneum Buys St. John's Church," October 31, 1905.

209. Wait, *History of St. John's Church*, 33–35.

210. Burr, *History of St. John's Church*, 29; Wait, *History of St. John's Church*, 2.

211. *Hartford Courant*, "Cornerstone of St. John's Removed," July 27, 1907; "Contents of Box Turned to Mould," September 26, 1907.

212. *Centennial Memorial*, 181–85; Trumbull, *Memorial History*, vol. 1, 400–1.

213. *Centennial Memorial*, 195.

214. Trumbull, *Memorial History*, vol. 1, 401.

215. *Hartford Courant*, "Old Landmark Doomed to Go," May 25, 1911.

216. *Centennial Memorial*, 199.

217. *Hartford Courant*, "Touro Hall," February 20, 1856; Trumbull, *Memorial History*, vol. 1, 401.

218. Trumbull, *Memorial History*, vol. 1, 401.

219. *Centennial Memorial*, 199.

220. *Hartford Courant*, "The South Baptist Church," May 5, 1852.

221. Ibid., "The Old Presbyterian Church," March 11, 1868.

222. Ibid., "New South Baptist Church," September 20, 1852; November 5, 1852; "Thomas Alexander Tefft," 94.

223. *Hartford Courant*, "South Baptist Church," April 20, 1854.

224. *Centennial Memorial* 207.

225. *Hartford Courant*, "First Baptist Church," December 3, 1853.

226. *Centennial Memorial*, 210.

227. Ibid., 208.

228. Bill Hosley, "Travelers' Founder: Hartford's 19th-Century Renaissance Man," *Hartford Courant*, May 23, 2012.

229. *Hartford Courant*, "New Church Edifice," April 2, 1856; *Centennial Memorial*, 211.

230. *Hartford Courant*, "New Church Edifice," April 2, 1856.

231. *Centennial Memorial*, 212–13.

232. *Hartford Courant*, "Pearl Street Church. Now Owned by William F. O'Neil, the Contractor," August 5, 1899.

233. *Hartford Courant*, "First Methodist Church 95 Years Old, Going Down," July 25, 1916.

234. Ibid., "New Methodist Episcopal Church in Asylum Street," April 13, 1860.

235. Ibid., "Passing of Old Methodist Church," April 15, 1911.

236. Ibid., "A.M.E. Zion Church May Go North," April 24, 1916; "Offer $55,000 for A.M.E. Church," April 25, 1916; "Pearl Street Church Discord," January 17, 1917; "A.M.E. Zion Church Not to Sell Site," July 29, 1920; July 20, 1921; March 7, 1922; April 28, 1922; May 15, 1922; January 19, 1923; "A.M.E. Zion Sale Held Up by Hill," July 10, 1923; "A.M.E. Zion Church to Arrange Lease," July 11, 1923; "A.M.E. Zion Church Granted Extension," July 2, 1925; "Church Makes Way for Fire Building," October 4, 1925.

237. Watt, *From Heresy toward Truth*, 9, 55.

238. *Hartford Courant*, "The Universalist Church," October 7, 1852.

239. Ibid., "Church of the Redeemer. Something About the New Decorations and Improvements," November 14, 1889.

240. Ibid., "New Business Block," April 13, 1899.

241. http://www.ushartford.com/lundy2.html.

242. http://www.ushartford.com/lundy3.html.

243. *Hartford Courant*, "The Unitarian Society," April 2, 1881

244. Ibid., "Unity Hall Has Been Transformed," September 26, 1914.

245. Walker, *History of the First Church*, 381.

BIBLIOGRAPHY

Andrews, Gregory E., and David F. Ransom. *Structures and Styles: Guided Tours of Hartford Architecture*. Hartford: Connecticut Historical Society and Connecticut Architecture Foundation, 1988.

Barber, John Warner. *Connecticut Historical Collections*. 2nd ed. New Haven, CT: Durrie & Peck and J.W. Barber, 1836.

Barnard, Henry. *School Architecture; or, Contributions to the Improvement of School-Houses in the United States*. New York: A.S. Barnes & Company, 1848.

Brooks, W.F. "The Fourth Congregational Church of Hartford." *Architecture* 42, no. 2 (August 1920): 238.

Burpee, Charles W. *First Century of the Phoenix National Bank of Hartford, Covering the Span Between the Federal Banking Epochs of 1814 and 1914*. Hartford, CT: Pheonix National Bank, 1914.

———. *One Hundred Years of Service: Being the History of the Hartford Fire Insurance Company*. Hartford, CT: Matthews-Northrup Works, 1910.

Burr, Nelson R. *A History of St. John's Church, Hartford, Connecticut, 1841–1941*. West Hartford, CT: St. John's Parish, 1941.

Campbell, John R. "Governor Talcott's Mansion and the City of Hartford's Claim." *Connecticut Magazine* 6, no. 5 (1900): 359–61.

Centennial Memorial of the First Baptist Church of Hartford, Connecticut, March 23 and 24, 1890. Hartford, CT: Press of Christian Secretary, 1890.

Close, F. Perry. *History of Hartford Streets*. Hartford: Connecticut Historical Society, 1969.

Contributions to the History of Christ Church, Hartford. Hartford, CT: Belknap & Warfield, 1895.

Derby, Alice Gray Southmayd. "The Riverside Cemetery: A Sketch of the Old Burying-Ground in Midletown." *Connecticut Quarterly* 2, no. 4 (1896): 385

Donaghue, Barbara. *Two Boxes, Three Trusts: The Legacy of Ethel Donaghue*. Hartford, CT: Patrick and Catherine Weldon Donaghue Medical Research Foundation, 1997.

Dunham, Austin C. *Reminiscences of Austin C. Dunham*. Hartford, CT: Case, Lockwood & Brainard Company, 1915.

The Evolution of a Building Lot. Hartford, CT: Travelers Insurance Company, 1913.

"Falling Section of the Steeple of the Pearl Street Church, Hartford," *Connecticut Magazine* 5, no. 12 (December, 1899): 646–7.

Gall, Henry R., and William George Jordan. *One Hundred Years of Fire Insurance: Being a History of the Aetna Insurance Company, Hartford, Connecticut, 1819–1919*. Hartford, CT: Aetna Insurance Company, 1919.

Grant, Ellsworth Strong, and Marion Hepburn Grant. *The City of Hartford, 1784–1894: An Illustrated History*. Hartford: Connecticut Historical Society, 1986.

Hale, Virginia. *A Woman in Business: The Life of Beatrice Fox Auerbach*. N.p.: Xlibris, 2008.

Half-Century History: Farmington Avenue Congregational Church. Harford, CT: Published by the church, 1901.

Hartford, Conn., as a Manufacturing, Business and Commercial Center; with Brief Sketches of its History, Attractions, Leading Industries, and Institutions. Hartford, CT: Hartford Board of Trade, 1889.

Hartford in 1912. Hartford, CT: *Hartford Post,* 1912.

Isham, Norman M., and Albert F. Brown. *Early Connecticut Houses.* Providence, RI: Preston and Rounds Company, 1900.

Kuckro, Anne Crofoot, et al. *Hartford Architecture: Hartford Architecture Conservancy Survey.* Hartford, CT: Hartford Architecture Conservancy, 1978–80.

Lilienthal, Hermann. *Christ Church Parish: A Century of its History and a Look into the Future. A Historical Sermon Preached in Christ Church, Hartford, Sunday Morning, February 9, 1902.* Hartford, CT: Case, Lockwood & Brainard Company, 1902.

Longstreth, Richard. *The Buildings of Main Street: A Guide to American Commercial Architecture.* Walnut Creek, CA: AltaMira Press, 2000.

Love, William DeLoss. *The Colonial History of Hartford.* Hartford: self-published, 1914.

Nenortas, Tomas. *Victorian Hartford.* Dover, NH: Arcadia Publishing, 2005.

———. *Victorian Hartford Revisited.* Dover, NH: Arcadia Publishing, 2007.

O'Donnell, James H. *History of the Diocese of Hartford.* Boston, MA: The D.H. Hurd Company, 1900.

O'Gorman, James F. *Henry Austin: In Every Variety of Architectural Style.* Middletown, CT: Wesleyan University Press, 2008.

Parker, Edwin Pond. *History of the Second Church of Christ in Hartford.* Hartford, CT: Belknap & Warfield, 1892.

Ransom, David F. *George Keller, Architect*. Hartford, CT: Hartford Architecture Conservancy and the Stowe-Day Foundation, 1978.

Rathbun, Julius. "Backward Glances at Hartford." *Connecticut Magazine* 5, no. 1 (January 1899): 42.

———. "Backward Glances at Hartford." *Connecticut Magazine* 5, no. 2 (February 1899): 104.

Remembering G. Fox & Co. A Brief History of Connecticut's Famous Department Store. Hartford: Connecticut Historical Society, 2012.

Sigourney, Lydia Huntley. *Letters of Life*. New York: D. Appleton and Company, 1867.

Steiner, Bernard C. *The History of Education in Connecticut*. Washington, D.C: Government Printing Office, 1893.

Sterner, Daniel. *A Guide to Historic Hartford, Connecticut*. Charleston, SC: The History Press, 2012.

Swift, David E. *Black Prophets of Justice: Activist Clergy Before the Civil War*. Baton Rouge: Louisiana State University Press, 1989.

"Thomas Alexander Tefft." *American Institute of Architects Quarterly Bulletin* 40, no. 2 (July 1910): 94.

Trumbull, J. Hammond, ed. *Memorial History of Hartford County*. 2 vols. Boston: Edward L. Osgood, 1886.

Twitchell, Willis I., ed. *Hartford in History. A Series of Papers by Resident Authors.* Hartford, CT: Press of the Plimpton Mfg. Company, 1907.

Verrett, Tamara. "Faith Congregational Church: 185 Years; Same People, Same Purpose." *Hog River Journal* 3, no. 3: 34–5.

Wait, Gary E. *A History of St. John's Church, 1841–1995*. West Hartford, CT: St. John's Church, 1996.

Walker, George Leon. *History of the First Church in Hartford, 1633–1883*. Hartford, CT: Brown & Gross, 1884.

Watt, Donald. *From Heresy Toward Truth: The Story of Universalism in Greater Hartford and Connecticut, 1821–1971*. Hartford, CT: Finlay Brothers, Inc., 1971.

Weaver, Glenn, and Michael Swift. *Hartford, Connecticut's Capital: An Illustrated History*. Sun Valley, CA: American Historical Press, 2003.

Weaver, Thomas S. *Historical Sketch of the Police Service of Hartford, from 1636 to 1801 from Authoritative Sources: Illustrating and Describing the Economy, Equipment and Effectiveness of the Police Force of To-Day; With Reminiscences of the Past, Including Some Notes of Important Cases*. Hartford, CT: Hartford Police Mutual Aid Association, 1901.

Weld, Stanley B. *The History of Immanuel Church, 1824–1967*. N.p.: Connecticut Printers Incorporated, 1968.

Woodward, P.H. *One Hundred Years of the Hartford Bank, Now the Hartford National Bank, of Hartford, Conn*. Hartford, CT: Case, Lockwood & Brainard Company, 1892.

INDEX

ABOUT THE AUTHOR

A lifelong resident of Connecticut, Daniel Sterner majored in history at Wesleyan University and earned a master's degree in Middle Eastern studies at the University of Chicago. He has been a guide at the Mark Twain and Harriet Beecher Stowe Houses in Hartford and the Webb-Deane-Stevens Museum in Wethersfield, Connecticut. His website, Historic Buildings of Connecticut (historicbuildingsct.com), and his previous book, *A Guide to Historic Hartford, Connecticut,* have both won awards from the Hartford Preservation Alliance.

Visit us at
www.historypress.net

....

This title is also available as an e-book